D0938215

WASHINGTON, D.C.

WASHINGTON, D.C.
BY ROAD

Rock
Creek

16th Street

29

Georgia Avenue

Tenleytown
(410 ft.)

Wisconsin Ave.

Connecticut Avenue

Rock Creek

Park Creek

16th Street

Massachusetts Ave.

1

Rhode Island Ave.

50

Canal Road

New York Avenue

Bladensburg Road

National
Arboretum

6th St.

I-395

Benning

Anacostia Rd.

295

Constitution Ave.

66

The Mall

River Park

East Capitol St.

Independence Ave.

Pennsylvania

395

East
Potomac
Park

Anacostia River

Fort Dupont
Park

Avenue

N

W ✦ E

S

Fort Stanton
Park

Capitol St.

South

295

Potomac River

FORESTS & PARKS

0   1   2   3   4

MILES

CELEBRATE THE STATES
WASHINGTON, D.C.

Dan Elish

BENCHMARK BOOKS

MARSHALL CAVENDISH
NEW YORK

Benchmark Books
Marshall Cavendish Corporation
99 White Plains Road
Tarrytown, New York 10591-9001

Library of Congress Cataloging-in-Publication Data
Elish, Dan
Washington, D.C. / Dan Elish.
p.   cm. — (Celebrate the states)
Includes bibliographical references (p.   ) and index.
Summary: Describes the geography, history, government, economy,
people, and culture of this city of contrasts.
ISBN 0-7614-0423-6 (lib. bdg.)
1. Washington, (D.C.)—Juvenile literature. [1. Washington (D.C.)] I. Title. II. Series.
F194.3.E45   1998   975.3—dc21   97-15042   CIP   AC

Maps and graphics supplied by Oxford Cartographers, Oxford, England

Photo Research by Ellen Barrett Dudley and Matthew J. Dudley

Cover Photo: *The Image Bank,* Anne Ripley

The photographs in this book are used by permission and through the courtesy of: *Photo Researchers, Inc.*:
Richard T. Nowitz, 6-7, 82, 114; Jeff Greenberg, 13; Mary Ann Hemphill, 23; Adams Morgan, 63; Mark
Burnett, 75; Fred Maroon, 80, 87, 138; Catherine Ursillo, 105; M. Borchi, 113; Gregory K. Scott, 121 (top);
John Kaprielian, 121 (bottom); Frans Lanting, 125; Walker Brothers, back cover. *UPI/Corbis-Bettmann:*
44, 45, 46, 53, 54, 69, 81, 130, 132 (top and bottom), 133 (top), 134. *The Image Bank:* Inner Light, 15;
John R. Ramey, 18; Pamela Zilly, 21, 107; Mitchell Funk, 59; James Meyer, 77; Lou Jones, 88-89; Tim Bieber,
100-101; Timothy Murphy, 117; Yellow Dogs Productions, 118. *Tom Stack & Associates:* Robert C. Simpson,
19; Mark Newman, 48-49; Brian Parker, 111; Thomas Kitchin, 124. *Photri:* Lani Novak Howe, 20, 66-67, 129;
T. Wachs, 60; John S. Attinello, 83; Henry T. Kaiser, 115. *Photri:* 16, 22, 25, 65, 72, 85, 110. *The Kiplinger
Collection:* 26-27, 36, 38. *Washington Historical Society:* 30, 33 (painting by Byron Leister). *Corbis-Bettmann:*
29, 37, 42, 78, 91, 92, 93, 98, 108- 109, 135. *Reuters/Corbis-Bettmann:* 76, 84, 95, 133 (bottom).
Springer/Corbis-Bettmann: 96. *The Washington Post:* Lucian Perkins, 64.

Printed in Italy

1   3   5   6   4   2

CONTENTS

WASHINGTON, D.C. IS...

Washington, D.C., is an exciting place to live.

"Watching President Clinton walk down Pennsylvania Avenue after he had been sworn in as President was one of the greatest thrills of my life."   —student Mary Jones

"Everyone who is important in the world today has to eventually find themselves here."   —teacher Ann O'Connell

Washington, D.C., is beautiful.

"I never lose the thrill of seeing the Capitol Building lit up at night."   —lawyer Barbara Eyman

"It's somewhat of a cliché, but the cherry blossoms in the spring around the tidal basin are breathtaking."
—businessman Ronald Gibbons

But Washington has turned into a tale of two cities: one for the wealthy, the other for the mostly black poor.

"This is the same city where the President of the United States lives and [the black community is] living in a war zone. How is he going to go overseas and tell other people how to live in peace, and he allows this to go on a few miles from the White House?"
—community advocate Mike Johnson

Indeed, Washington has come upon some hard economic times.

"Everything is broken. This isn't just a car that has run out of gas. There is something fundamentally wrong with the car. The gas pedal doesn't work and neither do the brakes."
—Department of Agriculture chief financial officer Anthony A. Williams

There is, however, great reason to hope for the future.

"Despite all its problems, Washington has so much potential. There's a great spirit here, a great energy, along with all those gorgeous monuments. This is where I want to be. This is where it's all happening."   —student Phyllis Hall

---

Washington is a city of grandeur and majesty. It is next to impossible to walk along its famous mall and not feel the power of our country's great history. The words of the timeless Gettysburg Address at the Lincoln Memorial or the thousands of names of lost soldiers carved into the black marble of the Vietnam Veterans Memorial are stirring testaments to our nation's past.

But there is another side to Washington, beyond the proud monuments, the White House, and Congress. Through years of mismanagement and money shortages, the city has been struggling for its economic survival. But Washington is fighting to change that. The federal government and the city are working together to find a way to ensure that the city receives the funding and leadership it deserves. With its long-term financial health now a priority, Washington's future looks bright.

1 THE NATION'S CAPITAL

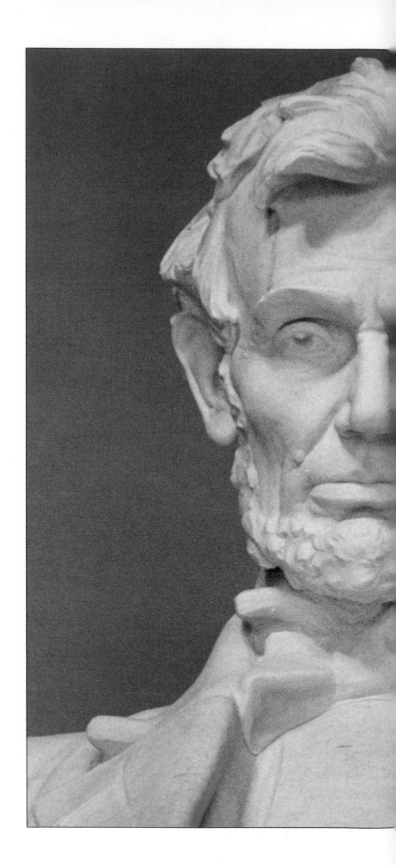

When most American citizens think of our nation's capital, they imagine the White House, marble monuments, and the dome of the Capitol. What most people don't know is that when Congress agreed on the site for its capital city in 1790, Washington, D.C., was what Thomas Jefferson, author of the Declaration of Independence and our country's third president, called "a swamp in the wilderness." Indeed, Washington of yesteryear was densely wooded and covered with marshland.

It took many years and much hard work to turn that swampy land into one of the world's most stunning cities. Located in a 68-square-mile nook between Maryland and Virginia, Washington is the capital of the world's only remaining superpower. Though its population is only 567,000 people, it is the home of senators, representatives, and diplomats from all over the globe. Virtually every critical world issue is debated in this small city on the banks of the Potomac River. One resident remarked, "Every day on the way to work a thought lurks in the back of my mind: that the president works down the block. And the vice president, too. Not to mention Congress. What can I say? It may sound corny but I find that very exciting. Washington is the center, not only of our country, but of the world."

Washington, D.C., seen from Arlington, Virginia, at dawn

GETTING AROUND WASHINGTON

It was George Washington himself who hand-picked Pierre L'Enfant, a brilliant French draftsman he had met at Valley Forge during the Revolutionary War, to be the architect of the city that would bear his name. But if you mention the name "L'Enfant" to a Washington-ian today, the famed Frenchman is liable to get mixed reviews.

"In theory," says Michael Richards, a D.C. journalist, "Washington was set up by L'Enfant to be easy to get around. In practice, though, unless you've lived here for a while it's nearly impossible to know where you are."

Of course, it may not be fair to blame L'Enfant for how Washington works today. As Leslie Pillner, a writer, put it, "It's hard to know whether it was L'Enfant's fault or if everybody who has come since messed up his plan."

The debate will undoubtedly continue for years to come. But it is certainly true that L'Enfant's original conception had its merits. L'Enfant imagined a city divided into four sections—the Northwest, Northeast, Southwest and Southeast—with the Capitol at its center. Two hundred years later that's exactly how the city is divided. The streets are numbered to the north and south and lettered to the east and west. Though this seems straightforward on paper, as Washington has grown, the system has gone somewhat awry. "Streets appear then disappear then appear again," one longtime resident says. "Take New York Avenue. Once you hit the White House, the street simply vanishes. It's frustrating."

Complicating things further are the traffic circles throughout the city. They were originally designed by L'Enfant as defensive emplacements where soldiers armed with cannons could stop invaders. But now, Michael Richards says, "All they succeed in doing is confusing people." A street reaches a traffic circle on one side and then disappears on the other.

Washington's odd streets frustrate the natives, especially in the spring, the city's prime tourist season. Don Wills, a local architect, remarked, "Each spring it happens. I get behind a guy with Iowa plates going about two miles an hour. This guy drives around Dupont Circle four times because he can't figure out which is the other side of P Street!"

Many natives prefer to get around town by the clean and efficient Metro, one of the world's most impressive subway systems. Unlike the city streets, the Metro's maps are extremely clear and easy to follow.

Rush hour in any large city brings heavy traffic, but in the capital traffic jams are legendary.

THE METRO

"The D.C. Metro is one of the wonders of the Western World," says reporter Frank Clines. "It's still as pristine now as it was when it opened twenty years ago."

Most Washingtonians would agree. The D.C. system is one of the most safe, efficient, and reliable—not to mention clean and comfortable—subways in America. Trains are constructed from graffiti-resistant material, and maps are easy to follow. Built deep underground because of Washington's swampy terrain, most Metro stops are entered through long escalators that can be almost as fun to ride as the train itself! (Take a look up the escalator at Dupont Circle. It's quite a sight.)

The Metro stands as a shining success in a city with a notoriously bad reputation for public services. In fact, given Washington's poor performance in delivering even the most basic services—from snowplowing to trash pick-up—it's amazing that their subway is so good. One resident said, "We may have our problems right now compared to some other cities. But this is one thing we've got over everyone!"

A BEAUTIFUL CITY

Everyone knows that our nation's capital is home to the Washington Monument, the 555-foot-tall white marble obelisk built to honor George Washington. What many people don't know is that a District of Columbia law states that no other building can be taller than this monument. "Washington has no skyscrapers blocking the sunlight," says Rick McAllister, a teacher. "It's refreshing in a major city." "There's a great feeling of openness," noted Leslie DeCrette, a tourist. "It's an altogether different feeling than New York or Chicago where everything is so built up."

All of that sunlight shines onto Pierre L'Enfant's wide avenues, many of which are graced by majestic trees, including "exotics"— Oriental ginkgoes, ailanthus, and Asiatic magnolias—imported to America from other countries. In 1805, President Jefferson did what he could to beautify the city by authorizing the planting of Lombardy poplars along Pennsylvania Avenue. In the mid-1960s, Lady Bird Johnson, the wife of the president, made the beautification of D.C. a top priority. It is partly a result of her efforts that Washington is home to 150 parks where flowers such as tulips, daffodils, and azaleas bloom. The district also supports a fair amount of wildlife. In the more secluded stretches of Rock Creek Park, some patient naturalists have run into raccoons, foxes, and opossums. In the spring, the bright songs of migrating warblers, thrushes, and finches fill the park.

Obviously, the most striking feature of the nation's capital is not its nature. What Washington is justifiably famous for are its noble monuments, magnificent museums, and stately architecture. Wash-

A yellow warbler relaxes in one of Washington's many parks.

ington is home to the Mall, one of the most gorgeous pieces of real estate in the country. Within walking distance lie the Lincoln Memorial, the Jefferson Memorial, the Capitol building, and the Washington Monument.

"But what I like best about this city," says one resident, "are the less famous spots. Have you ever walked down Massachusetts Avenue past Embassy Row? It sounds corny but it's a thrill to see all those stately buildings with guards out front, with the countries' flags flapping in the breeze."

The Washington Monument towers above all other buildings in the capital.

CLIMATE

"Washington's climate?" asks one longtime native. "Heat, heat and more heat. And don't get me started on the humidity! That's the weather in the nation's capital from May to September."

Indeed, in the summer, Washington is an extremely humid Southern town with long heat waves that reach into the nineties, which make its residents thankful for air-conditioning. "July and August are particularly terrible," one government employee notes. But at least it's not as bad as during the city's early days. In the nineteenth century, the summer brought malaria and yellow fever epidemics as the sun pounded on the mosquito-infested swamps.

A warm summer day turns the Washington Mall into a soccer field.

Lafayette Park covered by a winter snowfall

Winter in the district can be a mixed bag of cold days followed by warm spells. When nor'easters blow in, it's cold and wet. When the warm air from Bermuda waltzes through, it's windbreaker weather. Southerners at heart, most Washingtonians have trouble adapting to the occasional snowstorm. Schools shut down and people stay home from work in droves even if there's only snow in the forecast, let alone an inch or two on the ground.

Fall brings beautiful colors to Washington's many trees, but most residents agree that spring is the nicest time of year at the nation's

Georgetown in autumn. "Fall can be beautiful in Washington," says resident Leslie Decrette. "Don't let anyone tell you otherwise."

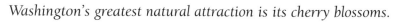

Washington's greatest natural attraction is its cherry blossoms.

capital. According to Michael Richards, "Spring is marvelous—and long. It tiptoes in in late February and lasts until mid-May. While Bostonians are still in down jackets and New Yorkers are getting chestnuts roasted on an open fire, D.C.'s weather is splendid."

ENVIRONMENTAL CONCERNS

Although it is hard to believe, during the summer of 1996, residents of our nation's capital were told to boil their drinking water! During those hot summer months, couples going out to fancy

restaurants sometimes brought their own bottled water along.

The problem was the city's aging water treatment plants and pipes. Years of neglect had allowed lead and dangerous bacteria to seep into Washington's water supply. To remedy the problem, the city added more chlorine to the water. Unfortunately, that chlorine made the water taste funny. And some residents complained that the chlorinated water created unpleasant fumes in their showers and made their hands wrinkle and chafe, the way they do after a long swim in a chlorinated pool.

As with many of the city's problems, Washington's water crisis stemmed from the district's economic troubles. For many years Washington didn't have the money to maintain some of its basic services. But emergencies often force governments to fork over cash. As Melissa Abernethy, a mother of two, said, "I'm glad the water problems are finally under control. Turning on my faucet last summer was more of an adventure than I wanted!"

The beautiful Potomac River was once heavily polluted.

The district has also run into problems with its recycling efforts. In the early 1990s, the city instituted curbside recycling, allowing residents to dump bottles and cans in large blue bins that stood outside their apartments and homes. But when the city became strapped for money in the late 1990s, curbside recycling was curtailed, forcing residents to lug their cans and bottles to a recycling center. "It's a big, fat pain," one Washingtonian complained. "I hate to admit it," Shawn Reynolds, an accountant, said, "but if I'm feeling lazy, I throw my bottles straight into the trash." Hopefully, when Washington gets its financial house in order, it will quickly reinstitute curbside recycling.

The city of Washington hasn't ignored all of its environmental problems, however. Though the Anacostia River remains polluted, a major clean-up effort in the 1970s has transformed the once dirty Potomac River into a beautiful waterway every Washington citizen can be proud of.

2 A CAPITAL IN A SWAMP

"**H**istory is rich in Washington," says painter Suzanne O'Neill. "You breathe it in every time you walk outside."

Indeed, it is nearly impossible to walk around downtown Washington and not run into a monument to our nation's past. Living in Washington you might work near the National Archives where the Declaration of Independence is kept on display. Or perhaps you would have a business meeting near the White House.

Though Washington is an American city that has borne witness to our nation's highest and lowest moments, the district also has a smaller history, a local history. It is a history of the people who lived in Washington long before Thomas Jefferson or Alexander Hamilton were born, a history of ordinary people who came to Washington in search of a better life.

EARLY SETTLERS

Native Americans called the Piscataways were the first people known to live in Washington. The Piscataways resided in villages surrounded by stake fences. They raised corn, squash, and other vegetables and fished the Potomac and Anacostia Rivers.

Though the Piscataways were peaceful, they were forced to waste valuable energy trying to steer clear of the warlike Iroquois Indians, who lived to the north. In the early 1600s when English colonists

The district's first residents, the Piscataway Indians, raised corn, squash, and other crops.

first appeared in Maryland and Virginia, the Piscataways tried to form alliances with the newcomers. Instead, they fell victim to smallpox, commonly known as "white man's disease." By 1680, most of the Piscataways had moved north and been absorbed into various Iroquois tribes. Though the Iroquois survived for many more years, they too were ultimately overrun by the whites.

In 1634, the land that is now the District of Columbia became part of England's Maryland Colony. Back then, most of Maryland was devoted to growing tobacco and was divided into large plantations that were worked by slaves. The first plantation within present-day Washington, Duddington Manor, was established in 1663. Life was very good for the rich plantation owners. While slaves did most of the work in the fields, the masters enjoyed horse races, fencing, and a calendar full of parties.

In 1751, the first of Washington's present-day neighborhoods was founded when Marylanders established Georgetown, named after King George II of England. Georgetown soon became a thriving port.

Old Georgetown was probably the largest tobacco port in the country toward the end of the eighteenth century.

CHOOSING THE CAPITAL

On July 4, 1776, the Continental Congress signed Thomas Jefferson's Declaration of Independence, a document that laid out the American colonies' grievances against the British Empire. In the course of the hard-fought Revolutionary War, General George Washington became a national hero. Eventually, the Constitution was written, and Washington was elected America's first president.

But there was one minor problem—where to put the capital? Though Philadelphia had served as the temporary capital, the Congress had also met in New York, Baltimore, Annapolis, Trenton, and York. Of course, nearly every city in the country wanted to be the nation's capital. After all, the mayors and citizens of each town correctly assumed that America's new capital would attract commerce and therefore money. It was an important and difficult decision. Finally, one congressman said, "We will make enemies no matter which city we choose. So let us build a completely new town for our national capital." America's founders recognized the historic opportunity that lay before them. Pierre L'Enfant wrote to George Washington, "No nation, perhaps, had ever before the opportunity offered them of deliberately deciding on the spot where their capital should be fixed."

But that choice was not easy. Though America did not fight the Civil War until 1861, the young country was already brimming with tensions between North and South. Thomas Jefferson, President Washington's secretary of state, was from Virginia and felt that the capital should be near his home state. George Washington, also from Virginia, wanted a capital near his home at Mount Vernon.

But many Northerners objected. Finally, Jefferson struck a deal with Alexander Hamilton, a northerner who headed the Treasury Department. Hamilton was worried about America's heavy war debts. Though the Revolutionary War had given America its cherished freedom, it had also cost a lot of money. Jefferson agreed to use his influence to persuade Congress to put up the cash to pay off the war debts, and in return Hamilton supported the site on the Potomac River for the new capital.

So the location of present-day Washington was picked. After Maryland and Virginia donated the land to create the capital, George Washington asked the nineteen property owners in the new district to give the federal government enough land to build the city's streets. He also asked if they would sell the government enough land for the president's home, a capitol, and various federal buildings at $66.66 an acre. The owners agreed, knowing full well that the property values of the land they held onto would skyrocket when the district became a thriving city.

With the land secured, President Washington got in touch with Pierre L'Enfant.

PIERRE L'ENFANT

Like many Frenchmen of his day, Pierre L'Enfant, an art student in Paris, had volunteered to fight on the side of the American rebels in the Revolutionary War. L'Enfant first came to George Washington's attention at Valley Forge, where he drew sketches to keep busy during the long winter. After the war, L'Enfant worked as an architect and an engineer in New York. (L'Enfant was also responsible

Pierre L'Enfant had the imagination to foresee a thriving, elegant capital city in the midst of mud, Indian trails, and overgrown forest.

for designing the Purple Heart, a medal awarded to wounded American soldiers.) When he heard about the new capital, he immediately dashed off a letter to Washington asking if he could take part in the planning. Washington was impressed by his enthusiasm. L'Enfant arrived at the city in 1791, eager to get to work.

With the assistance of Andrew Ellicott, a surveyor from Pennsylvania, and his assistant, Benjamin Banneker, a black astronomer and mathematician, L'Enfant traveled the countryside surveying the land. Three weeks later he made public his plan for a city full of monuments, a presidential palace, a statue of George Washington, and, at the very center on a spot called Jenkins Hill, the Capitol. Connecting the Capitol and the president's home would be a ceremonial boulevard (today's Pennsylvania Avenue). Extending westward from the Capitol would be a "vast esplanade" (today's Mall, home of the Smithsonian museums and various monuments).

But L'Enfant's plans seemed too ambitious for most Washingtonians. His call for broad streets, 100 to 110 feet wide, infuriated landowners who had been persuaded to give up their property for cheap. (Most infuriating was Pennsylvania Avenue, which was to be 400 feet wide!) L'Enfant also proved uncompromising. Once he committed his ideas to paper, he refused to change them. The last straw came when Daniel Carroll, heir to Duddington Manor, began constructing a house that would block one of the Frenchman's planned avenues. In a fit of rage, L'Enfant ordered the house torn down. There was nothing George Washington could do but relieve the talented architect of his duties. Though Congress offered him $2,500 for his efforts (no small sum in those days), the furious L'Enfant refused. The Frenchman's plans were still used, however, with minor modifications. Having never received a single cent for all his hard work, L'Enfant died in poverty in 1825.

THE NEW CAPITAL

Moving the U.S. capital to Washington in 1800 was fairly simple. Back then, the American government was not yet burdened by excessive bureaucracy. In fact, the young country employed only 126 people! On November 2, John Adams became the first resident of the White House.

JOHN HENRY BUILDS THE WASHINGTON MONUMENT

Back in the 1800s when America was wild and untamed, a man named John Henry roamed the countryside, working on railroads. Henry was an enormous fellow. He stood twenty feet tall barefoot and was thirty feet wide.

One day in 1888, he strode into Washington. He had a bone to pick with the president. "President Cleveland," he said gruffly. "I was workin' the railroad down Georgia way and I hear tell that the monument to George Washington isn't finished. What's the delay?"

President Cleveland looked up and up and up at the mighty man and swallowed hard. "Well, Mr. Henry," he stammered. "I don't rightly know. Come with me and we'll ask the Senate."

So President Cleveland led John Henry to the Capitol. (They attracted quite a crowd. It's not every day a twenty-foot-tall, thirty-foot-wide gentleman visits our nation's capital.) "Why isn't the Washington Monument finished?" Cleveland asked the Senate.

"Got me," a senator from New Jersey said. "Let's ask the House of Representatives!"

And they did. But the House of Representatives wanted to ask the Supreme Court. And the Supreme Court wanted to ask the foreign ambassadors. Pretty soon everyone in town was yapping about the problem, but nothing was being done.

Well, that didn't suit a man of action like John Henry. The next day he strapped two tons of marble onto his back, scaled the side of the famous monument, and completed it himself. All in two hours!

"How'd ya do it so fast?" someone asked the giant.

Henry shrugged. "You'd be surprised what you can accomplish when you work instead of argue." Then he smiled. "People in Washington might learn something from that!"

Irish builder James Hoban designed the White House after winning a competition. (Thomas Jefferson was an anonymous loser.) The first cornerstone was laid on October 13, 1792.

The Washington of the early 1800s was not nearly as magnificent as the Washington of today. There was only one recognizable street, today's New Jersey Avenue. Pennsylvania Avenue did not yet exist. Instead, the space between the president's house and Congress was covered with alder bushes. Cows grazed by the uncompleted streets, hogs ran in the mud, and cornfields grew by homes. One visiting New Yorker remarked, "We only need more houses, cellars, kitchens, scholarly men, amiable women, and a few other such trifles to possess a perfect city."

THE WAR OF 1812

By 1810, conditions weren't much improved. Washington remained a half-built city. To add to America's troubles, the young country was soon at war again with England, this time over control of the high seas. The powerful British navy easily overwhelmed American ships, and on August 24, 1814, English troops invaded Washington, torching the White House and many other unfinished public buildings. But America eventually rallied and won the war. In 1815, the nation had to start from scratch and build Washington up from rubble.

The British burned much of the capital during the War of 1812.

THE CIVIL WAR

Though Washington's population rose from fourteen thousand in 1800 to around thirty-five thousand by 1832, Americans were hardly flocking to the hot and humid city. Much of Washington was still marshland, and disease-carrying mosquitoes were a serious problem. L'Enfant's wide avenues remained unfinished. One English writer noted in 1828 upon seeing the Capitol, "Everybody knows that Washington has a Capitol, but the misfortune is that the Capitol wants a city. There it stands, reminding you of a general without an army, only surrounded and followed by a

In 1832, open fields still surrounded the Capitol.

parcel of ragged little boys, for such is the appearance of the dirty, straggling, ill-built houses which lie at the foot of it."

The residents of those "ill-built" houses were more often than not the eleven thousand free black men and women who by 1860 had migrated from the South and worked in largely menial jobs. Washington also allowed slavery. In fact, the city was a center for the slave trade, causing one man to observe, "You call this the land of liberty, and every day things are done in it at which the despotisms of Europe would be horror-struck and disgusted. . . . In no part of the earth . . . is there so great, so infamous a slave market, as in the metropolis, in the seat of government of this nation which prides itself on freedom."

Indeed, slavery was the issue that drove America to the Civil War, a conflict that had an enormous effect on Washington. During the war, the city became the major supply depot and hospital camp for the Union army. Food and water ran low. Typhoid and dysentery epidemics ravaged the town. Hundreds of private homes, churches, and warehouses were used as army barracks and hospitals. Ovens were even set up in the Capitol basement!

When the exhausting war was finally won by the North in 1865, Washington was in shambles. Washington's population had risen to one hundred thousand, overwhelming the city. Poor people, many of them newly freed slaves, migrated from the South and settled in shacks. These new citizens had been agricultural workers and had few skills to use in a town where government was the main employer.

In 1870, a builder named Alexander Shepherd was appointed to Washington's Board of Public Works. Drawing on funds allocated

WE'LL FIGHT FOR UNCLE ABE

We'll Fight for Uncle Abe praises Civil War generals Grant and McClellan, while expressing the growing popularity of "Uncle Abe" Lincoln. Although the actual fighting had been taking place in Virginia and points farther south, it was Washington, D.C., that symbolized the Union's struggle against the Confederacy.

Words by C. E. Pratt
Music by Frederick Buckley

Way down in old Var- gin - ny, I sup- pose you all do know, They have

tried to bust the Un - ion, But they find it is no go. The

Yan- kee boys are start - ing out, The Un - ion for to save, And we're

go - ing down to Wash - ing- ton To fight for Un - cle Abe.

Chorus

Rip, Rap, Flip, Flap, Strap your knap - sack on your back, For

we're goin' down to Wash - ing - ton to fight for Un - cle Abe.

There is General Grant at Vicksburg,
Just see what he has done,
He has taken sixty cannon
And made the Rebels run,
And next he will take Richmond,
I'll bet you half a dollar,
And if he catches General Johnson,
Oh won't he make him holler. (Chorus)

The season now is coming
When the roads begin to dry;
Soon the Army of the Potomac
Will make the Rebels fly,
For General McClellan, he's the man,
The Union for to save;
Oh! Hail Columbia's right side up,
And so's your Uncle Abe. (Chorus)

You may talk of Southern chivalry
And cotton being king,
But I guess before the war is done
You'll think another thing;
They say that recognition
Will the Rebel country save,
But Johnny Bull and Mister France
Are 'fraid of Uncle Abe. (Chorus)

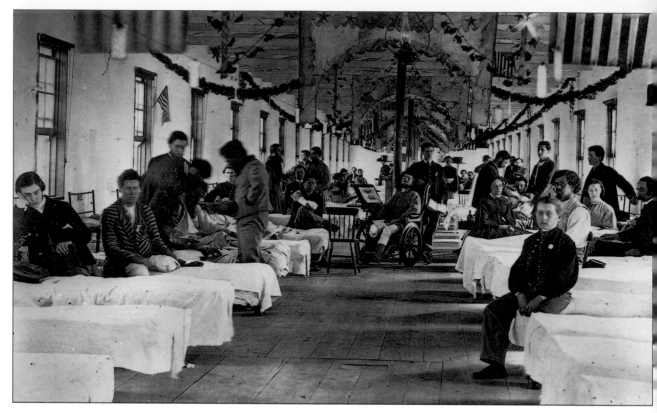

Some three thousand Union soldiers lived in the Capitol during the Civil War. The building came to be known as the Big Tent.

by Congress, Shepherd organized crews of poor workers, who paved roads, planted trees, and dug sewers. As the city gradually became more livable, it attracted foreign investment. But Shepherd spent more money than he had been allotted and left the city $18 million in debt. With that, Congress decided that Washington was unable to manage its internal affairs and in 1874 put the city under the auspices of three commissioners appointed by the president. Washingtonians had suddenly lost the right to vote, and the capital of the "land of the free" was now ruled like a colony.

FACING THE TWENTIETH CENTURY

World War I affected Washington in much the same way as the Civil War had—the population rose dramatically, this time to 450,000, and shortages again struck the city. The 1920s brought a building boom (many monuments were completed, including the Lincoln Memorial in 1922), and the Great Depression of the 1930s caused President Franklin Roosevelt to initiate a program he called the New Deal, which created thousands of government jobs for out-of-work Americans and expanded the size of the Washington bureaucracy and population yet again.

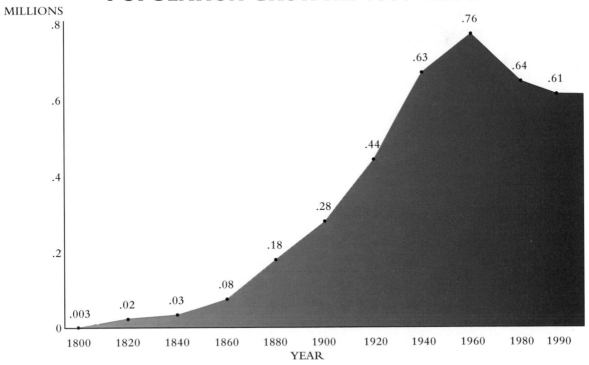

POPULATION GROWTH: 1800–1990

As the United States entered World War II in 1941, many Washingtonians, mostly black, still lived in poor conditions. In 1944, Senator Theodore Bilbo became chairman of the district committee that oversaw Washington. Bilbo was a virulent segregationist who once opposed an antilynching law and proposed a bill that would have deported twelve million blacks to Liberia. Though known as "the Mayor of Washington," Bilbo was so racist that he did whatever he could to deny the district funds. Needless to say, black Washingtonians did not thrive with Theodore Bilbo in charge.

African Americans march for the ouster of Senator Theodore Bilbo, who once proposed a bill in Congress that called for the deportation of 12 million blacks to Liberia.

Civil rights leader Dr. Martin Luther King Jr. waves to the crowd after delivering his famous "I Have a Dream" speech.

In the 1950s, after Bilbo's death, Washington's district committee was taken over by another white segregationist, John L. McMillan of South Carolina. Not much better than his predecessor, "Johnny Mack" refused to even hold hearings on various proposals for Washington self-government. Thus, into the 1960s Congress continued to run Washington without much thought for the welfare of its citizens. As one journalist put it, "Today's speeches about the glories of democracy should always be followed by the words, 'except in Washington.' The fact that those who live in the seat of democracy do not enjoy its basic prerogatives is quite literally incredible."

THE 1968 RIOTS

When the great civil rights leader Martin Luther King Jr. was gunned down in April 1968, anger in black communities across America boiled over. In Washington, for three horrible days up to 20,000 people broke windows, looted stores, and set fires, causing President Lyndon Johnson to call in federal troops. But even the presence of the army couldn't contain the rioters as store after store was destroyed.

By the time it was over, 6,300 people had been arrested and twelve had died. The value of lost property was estimated at $15 million. Businesses that had sustained many black neighborhoods for years had been destroyed. The riots caused many middle-class people to move out of the city altogether.

The 1968 riots are still a dividing point in the city's history. People talk about the city "before the riots" and "after the riots." One young black woman said, "It was a defining moment in my life. Before Dr. King's death I had a feeling that things were going to work, integration would work, people would get along, racism was under control. Then I realized it wasn't going to work."

HOME RULE AT LAST

Something had to give. In 1965, President Lyndon Johnson fought to give the citizens of Washington home rule but was voted down by the same vocal minority of Southern segregationists who had always stood in the way.

But after the assassination of civil rights leader Martin Luther King Jr., horrible riots broke out in the city. The anger of the black community was not lost on most white leaders, and they stepped up efforts to give the city's residents back their basic rights. In 1970, Washingtonians regained the right to elect a delegate to the House of Representatives. In 1973, Congress gave Washington the right to elect its own mayor, which was approved by district residents a year later. Finally, the district had won home rule and with it the right to make decisions for itself.

3 A CITY IN TRANSITION

The Capitol of the United States

Washington, D.C., is an odd creature. From the late 1800s until the 1970s, the city was ruled by Congressional committee. Even when Washington finally won the right to home rule in 1974 and was allowed to elect its own mayor, it was still partly deprived of the ability to tax and raise revenue that most other American cities take for granted. The result has been disastrous. After years of living above its means, the city is deep in debt. One local reporter remarked, "For years Washington has been a ward of the federal government which neglects it."

Today, Washington is struggling to stand on its own two feet and find a way to achieve financial stability.

INSIDE GOVERNMENT

We all know that Washington is the home of our federal government, which is divided into three branches: the executive (the president), the legislative (the Senate and House of Representatives), and the judicial (the courts). Indeed, most American states and cities have a similar governing structure. But Washington's local government is unique. In 1995, President Bill Clinton established a "control board," a committee that was given authority to oversee the city's poorly managed finances. Though the control board now has the real power, the mayor of Washington remains an influential figure.

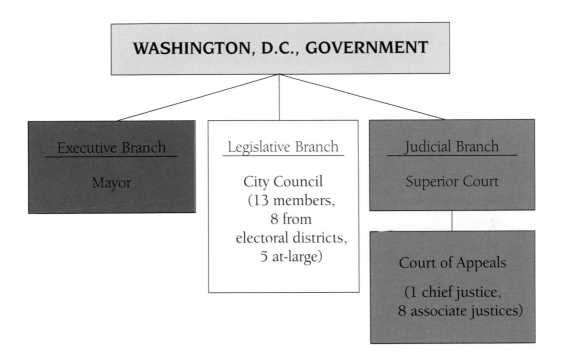

WASHINGTON, D.C., GOVERNMENT

Executive Branch

Mayor

Legislative Branch

City Council
(13 members,
8 from
electoral districts,
5 at-large)

Judicial Branch

Superior Court

Court of Appeals

(1 chief justice,
8 associate justices)

The Mayor. In Washington, the mayor is elected to a four-year term, with no term limits. The mayor appoints heads of departments such as police and fire and submits a budget for a vote by the city council. Since 1995, the mayor's budget also has to pass muster with the control board, which has the final say on how every cent is spent in the city. All money for services such as police, garbage collection, the awarding of contracts for new buildings— everything that a city needs to run— is subject to the control board's seal of approval. Washingtonians know full well where the real power in the city now rests. Some homeowners in Washington's wealthy Third Ward put signs in front of their homes that read: "Control Board. If schools are not your priority this house is for sale!"

Before the control board was created, the mayor of Washington had more power. The key player in the history of modern-day Washington is the city's second mayor, Marion Barry Jr., who was first elected in 1978.

Barry was born in 1936 and grew up in Memphis, Tennessee, in a poor family with nine brothers and sisters. A good student, Barry eventually found his way to LeMoyne College in South Memphis, where he become active in student government and the civil rights movement. In his senior year, he took part in a Memphis bus deseg-regation case.

In 1960, he became head of a civil rights organization called the Student Nonviolent Coordinating Committee and addressed that year's Democratic Presidential Convention. He told the delegates, "For 350 years, the American Negro has been sent to the back door in education, housing, employment, and the rights of citizenship at the polls." These were bold words for a young man addressing a hall full of mostly white establishment politicians.

Barry made his way to Washington, D.C., in 1965 and almost immediately organized a black boycott of a city bus line that was planning a fare increase. Hard on the heels of that victory, Barry became one of the leading advocates for home rule and was soon well-known and respected in the district's black communities.

As mayor he initially earned the good will of the entire city, including the wealthier whites, who saw in him a superb politi-cian who might be able to get the city's spiraling budgets under control. But throughout the 1980s, Barry, with no conservative opposition, championed a liberal philosophy in which the govern-ment provided jobs and services and paid little attention to the

In 1966, future mayor Marion Barry stated, "We want to free D.C. from our enemies: the people who make it impossible for us to do anything about lousy schools, brutal cops, slumlords, welfare investigators who go on midnight raids, employers who discriminate in hiring, and a host of other ills that run rampant through our city."

city's budget or physical condition. Today, Barry admits that his emphasis may have been a bit off. "My focus was on social services, jobs and education," he says. "In retrospect, we should have paid more attention to roads and bridges."

Either through lack of funds or poor management, under Barry's watch the quality of the city's social services continued to decline dramatically. Barry remained a popular mayor, however, throughout the 1980s, until he was convicted of drug possession. In what became a national embarrassment to the city, a videotape of Barry purchasing crack cocaine was broadcast on televisions throughout the country.

When his brief prison term was over, Marion Barry went about the business of resurrecting his political career. Though he had lost the support of the white neighborhoods, he was still immensely popular in the black parts of the city. He moved into the African-American ward 8, won a council seat, and, in 1994, defeated the

Marion Barry campaigns in 1994 to win his old job back.

incumbent mayor, Sharon Pratt Kelly, in the Democratic primary. He then easily won the general election.

Now the city is back in his hands. Having kicked his drug habit, he is eager to lead Washington to a brighter future. Is he the right man for the job? That remains to be seen. Some residents are skeptical: "What kind of citizenry would reelect a mayor who went to jail for doing drugs?" one asked. But a member of the control board had a slightly more balanced view, "Mr. Barry is a tremendous politician," he said. "But he's a lot like nuclear power. On a good day, he can light the city. On a bad day, he can blow it up."

The City Council. Washington is divided into eight districts, each of which elects one member to the city council. Five additional councilpeople are elected in a citywide vote. Like the mayor, the city council is under the thumb of the Congressional control board, which must approve everything the council does. But the city council does get the first crack at the mayor's budget each year before sending it along to Congress.

Judicial. The district has two levels of courts. The lower level, called the Superior Court, is broken into several different divisions that include family, criminal, civil, and housing courts. The highest court in the district is the Court of Appeals. All judges in Washington are picked by the president, who chooses from a list of three names given to him by a local judicial appointment commission. All judges serve fifteen years, and unless there is misconduct they are usually reappointed.

Unlike the rest of Washington's government, the district's court system is independent of Congressional control. Of course, decisions can be appealed to the Supreme Court, but Congress has no authority to override a local Washington court decision.

NEW COLUMBIA

Until recently, there was a vocal group of Washingtonians who supported an amendment to the United States Constitution to make the nation's capital the state of "New Columbia." Though most district politicians are Democrats, every two years one or two of the city council seats were won by members of the "statehood" party. For a while it seemed as though there was a chance that the district would become our fifty-first state. President Clinton endorsed the idea in his 1992 election bid, and civil rights activist Jesse Jackson sat poised to be one of New Columbia's first senators. But opposition to the idea was always strong among the Republican Party, which did not want to admit another Democratic state into Congress. And when Washington's financial crisis hit a boiling point in 1995, statehood was deemed unworkable. As one member of the city council said, "There was no way Congress would vote to let us be our own state when we were going broke."

ECONOMIC WOES

Washington's economic picture over the past several years has been bleak at best. The reasons for this are complex. But most Washingtonians would agree that when Congress granted the district home rule it imposed what the *New York Times* called "a bad financial and political deal on the city." According to Mayor Barry, "Those of us who were fighting for home rule were so anxious to get some degree of freedom, we didn't examine what it was. We inherited a mess."

Indeed, there are many obstacles that make governing Washington successfully next to impossible. The city is not allowed to tax the commuters who make up two-thirds of the district's work force. It cannot tax the 43 percent of the property within its borders that is owned by the government, diplomatic missions, or non-profit institutions. The city must pay for a variety of "safety-net" social service programs like Medicaid, the cost of which it splits with the federal government (most other cities pay nothing for Medicaid). In 1974, the district's Medicaid bill was around $17 million. In the past twenty years that number has ballooned to around $200 million!

1992 GROSS DISTRICT PRODUCT: $32 BILLION

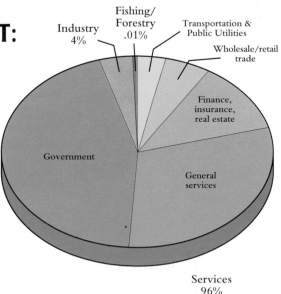

Industry 4%

Fishing/ Forestry .01%

Transportation & Public Utilities

Wholesale/retail trade

Finance, insurance, real estate

Government

General services

Services 96%

Add into the mix that Washington is a government town. Hundreds of thousands of people are employed by Uncle Sam—in jobs ranging from president to garbage collector. Most people move to Washington to work for the federal government, and the city does not attract many small businesses. Once a business leaves the city limits for Maryland or Virginia, it is a complete financial loss to the district. James Gibson, the city's planning commissioner, explains, "If you move out of New York to Westchester County [a suburb, also in New York state] you still pay taxes to the state, which kicks back some to the city of New York in the form of state aid. Here, if you move, it's a 100 percent loss to Washington."

Washington's efforts throughout the years to even the playing field have largely failed. One of the city's main gripes has always been the lack of a commuter tax. But reporter Frank Clines says, "To pass a commuter tax would need the cooperation of Congress and Congress just picks on Washington. And there's no way that Virginia and Maryland would let it pass." Though it's hard to blame the senators of Washington's border states for wanting to spare their citizens another tax, this impasse has deprived the district of a vital source of income that every other major city in the country takes for granted. (Because of Washington's inability to tax commuters, the city does have a high restaurant tax of 10 percent—still not enough to balance their books). Fred Cooke, the city's former chief lawyer, remarked, "I think you could bring

The District of Columbia is unable to tax the many thousands of commuters who drive into Washington to work.

the smartest person from the Harvard School of Government down here, and he couldn't make this thing work."

WANT SNOW CLEARED? GOOD LUCK!

As Washington's economy has crumbled, its ability to provide its citizens with basic services such as garbage collection has declined dramatically. For example, the winter of 1995 brought record blizzards to Washington, but days passed before streets were plowed. "I live right across the border in Takoma, Maryland," Skip

A Southern city at heart, Washington is ill-prepared to deal with snowstorms.

PARKING TICKETS

Despite the decay of virtually all of the city's services over the past several years, there is one department that is notorious for doing an excellent job: the special force of the police assigned to give out parking tickets. "Washington is unbelievable in that way," says writer Leslie Pillner. "You leave your car parked in an illegal space for thirty seconds and you've got a ticket." In fact, many Washingtonians lost all patience during the 1995 blizzard, when cars that were buried deep in snow because of poor city snow-removal service were ticketed!

"This city is unbelievable!" one resident fumed. "My car is buried under snow for a week and by the time it melts I owe the city two hundred bucks!"

Aronson, a journalist says. "The streets on the Washington side were covered with snow while ours were plowed pretty much right away." Though part of the problem was that Washington, a Southern town, was not equipped to deal with so much snow, the main issue was its poor economic situation. "Local plowing companies refused to work for the city of Washington," one native said. "They were afraid they may never get paid."

The further one looks into the inner workings of the nation's capital, the bleaker the picture becomes. According to the *New York Times*, nearly a third of the city's sixteen water-pumping fire trucks are kept out of service on any given day for lack of funds. AIDS testing is routinely halted to save money. Between 1991 and 1994, the city's public works budget was cut by $95 million, leading to disrepair on streets and bridges. Indeed, Washington has much more than its share of potholes.

The police department has suffered as well. Two policemen who work in Washington's poor Eighth Ward admitted that supplies were so short they were lucky to have a car that ran. They also said that their station had only one typewriter, and it was often without a ribbon. "If you want to type your reports," one said, "you've got to bring your own."

CRIME AND DRUGS

Washington's economic difficulties have taken a serious toll on the city. In the district's poorer neighborhoods, which are largely African-American, crime is a significant problem. Thirteen-year-old Markeisha Richardson said, "We had two people shot in my building once. And the other day, some boys jumped out of a car and started shooting. They looked younger than me. I just don't know why life is so crazy sometimes."

In the 1980s, Washington was dubbed "Murder Capital USA." Today, while murder rates in many other cities are declining, Washington's is still rising. Of course, the reasons are complex. The Washington police force has been underfunded. Public education has been poorly run for years, and inadequate education can often lead young people to give up. Then there are drugs. "The influx of the drug called crack made people crazy," a government worker says. "That set law enforcement back."

Indeed, crack cocaine, the drug of choice in poor neighborhoods across the country in the late 1980s and early 1990s, contributed greatly to Washington's soaring crime rate. With drugs come drug dealers and drug gangs fighting and often dying for turf.

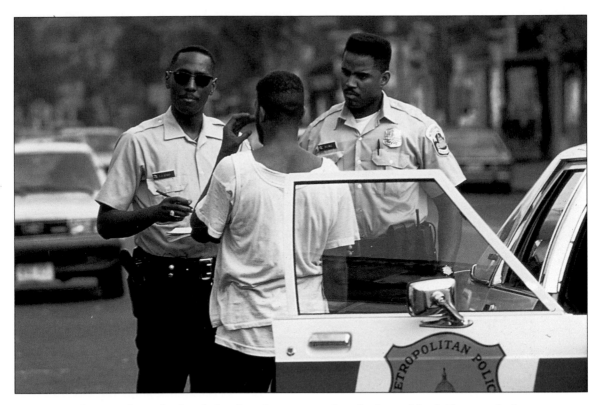
Washington's underfunded police department has had trouble dealing with the crime and drug problems that plague the city.

But out-of-towners should not be afraid of visiting. Though Washington's tourist industry has suffered a bit in recent years, there is little evidence that the district as a whole is unsafe. "I've lived here for twenty years," says Neil Feinburg, a Washington stockbroker. "And the threat of crime doesn't cross my mind especially." Though crime has encouraged some residents to leave town for the suburbs, many Washingtonians remain happy right where they are. Ivan Reik, a construction worker, remarked, "The district has good neighborhoods and bad neighborhoods. Sure, there's crime, but don't forget that most of Washington is pretty

ROSA LEE

In 1994, the *Washington Post* published a series of stories by Leon Dash, called "Rosa Lee's Story: Poverty and Survival in Washington."

For four days, Post readers learned about Rosa Lee, a black woman who lived in one of Washington's poorest neighborhoods. A mother of eight children by six different men, dependent on welfare and addicted to drugs for a large part of her adult life, Rosa Lee did what she could "to support her family." She shoplifted on a regular basis, pedaled heroin, and also turned many of her children onto drugs.

In Dash's stories, Rosa Lee is not portrayed as a villain. Rather, she is seen as a whole person—someone who was raised by a domineering mother, was illiterate (and therefore unable to obtain a decent job), and ultimately died of AIDS.

To read about Rosa Lee is to feel appalled at one moment and sympathetic the next—appalled when she spends her welfare check on drugs but sympathetic when she is brutally beaten by one of her husbands. Like many Washingtonians who live in poverty, Rosa Lee is neither entirely responsible for her circumstances nor entirely free from blame.

While many famous and powerful people work in Washington, D.C., the majority of the people who live there are often forgotten. In bringing to light the story of one poor black woman, Leon Dash helped others better appreciate the complicated problems facing the urban poor.

Washingtonians and tourists alike enjoy the city's varied activities, such as the White House Easter Egg Roll.

beautiful. I walk to work every day through Rock Creek Park and I've never gotten mugged."

Despite all the problems, many Washingtonians are hopeful that their city will be able to turn itself around. Leaders in the district and the federal government, Democrat and Republican alike, are working together to get Washington back on its economic feet.

4 TALE OF TWO CITIES

Historically, our nation's capital has been one of the most racially divided cities in the country. Although it was the first American city with a black majority (according to the 1960 census), Washington has been accurately referred to as "the last colony," because its government was firmly controlled by a white, often segregationist, Congress. To this day any understanding of the nation's capital must include an understanding of long-term resentments between the majority black population and the minority white population who, for so many years, held the power in the city.

RACISM AT THE NATION'S CAPITAL

In 1890, a tall plantation owner and United States senator named John Tyler explained why Washingtonians had lost the right to vote: "The historical fact is simply this. That the Negroes came into this District from Virginia and Maryland and from other places . . . and they took possession of a certain part of the political power of this District . . . and there was but one way to get out—so Congress thought . . . and that was to deny the right of suffrage [the vote] entirely to every human being in the District and have every office here controlled by appointment instead of by election . . . in order to get rid of this load of Negro suffrage that was flooded in upon them."

Senator Tyler's words sum up the problems blacks in Washington, D.C., faced for years. On the border of the South, the city was under the thumb of Southern senators and representatives— people who were unsympathetic, to say the least, to the plight of the black citizenry. As more and more African Americans migrated north to the district, the conditions in which they lived deteriorated. The influential African-American leader Malcolm X visited the city in 1941 and observed, "I was astounded to find in the nation's capital, just a few blocks from Capital Hill, thousands of Negroes

In the 1940s, many African Americans still lived in decrepit housing.

living . . . in dirt-floor shacks along unspeakably filthy lanes with names like Pig Alley and Goat Alley." He also noted, "I saw other Negroes better off; they lived in blocks of rundown red brick houses. The old 'Colonial' railroaders had told me about Washington having a lot of 'middle class' Negroes . . . who were working as laborers, janitors, porters, guards, taxi-drivers, and the like. For the Negro in Washington, mail carrying was a prestige job."

Indeed, these middle-class blacks had always been an enormous source of pride among Washington's African Americans. How upsetting, then, to be deprived of the basic right to vote and have Congressional representation that every other American citizen enjoyed. What resentment built up over years and years of mistreatment by Congressional committees, which used the district as a means to grant patronage jobs.

When the city won home rule in 1974, many blacks were thrilled to finally have control of the first black majority city, affectionately dubbed "Chocolate City," after a 1940s song that claimed: "Hey, we didn't get our 40 acres and a mule, but we did get you, Chocolate City. You don't need the bullet when you've got the ballot." But Washington's poor economy and stubborn social problems have rubbed salt in the wounds of racial issues that, in a better world, would have quietly gone away years ago.

RACE ISSUES TODAY

When the control board effectively took over the district's local government in 1995, many white Washingtonians were happy that steps were being taken to confront the city's fiscal woes. But many blacks were not pleased. They viewed the control board as a means for whites to regain control of the city. Indeed, any issue in Washington has to be handled with the utmost sensitivity in regard to race. As Representative Thomas M. Davis of Virginia put it, "The difficulty has been every time Congress tried to intervene [in the affairs of the city], people yell home rule or racism." The lack of understanding between whites and blacks was typified in a T-shirt that found its way onto the backs of many young African Americans in the early 1990s: "It's a black thing, you wouldn't understand."

A crime in 1992 demonstrated how race pervades every part of D.C. life. Tom Barnes was a young, white congressional aide who moved to the city in 1991 to work for Alabama senator Richard Shelby. On January 11, 1992, Barnes went out to buy some coffee and was shot and killed. Senator Shelby was furious, and a city-wide manhunt was organized to catch the murderer. The search produced Lloyd Hardy, a black youth, who was soon released for lack of evidence. Hardy's grandmother told the *Washington Post*: "They threw out the net and said, 'Find somebody' and they found somebody—another black youth. . . . As long as they fish out and get a black child, that satisfies them."

Senator Shelby still wasn't satisfied and soon forced the district to hold a referendum on capital punishment. Black Washingtonians, many who probably believed in capital punishment, resented a Southern white senator telling them what to do. As a result, Shelby's initiative was soundly defeated. John Wilson, a black city council-man, remarked, "I'm in favor of the death penalty but I don't want someone who we didn't elect ordering us to take the vote."

Many middle-class blacks have left Washington for suburbs such as Mt. Rainier, Maryland, because they prefer its small-town feel.

FLIGHT OF THE BLACK MIDDLE CLASS

For years, Washington has been home to a thriving black middle class. But recently many better-off African-American Washingtonians have moved to the suburbs. Nearly fifty thousand blacks moved out of the district in the 1980s. During the same period, the city's white population increased by nearly eight thousand. "It's strange," says Leslie McGuire, a teacher. "But D.C. is one of the only American cities that has become whiter while growing poorer."

Why have these middle-class blacks decided to put down roots elsewhere? Mostly, for the better quality of life the suburbs afford. A resident of Mount Rainier, one of the new black suburbs, says: "I wouldn't come back into the city because of all the problems that have cropped up since I left, basically the poor city services. I love Mount Rainier. It's like a little town with a mayor you can call up and who will come over on his bike."

Despite their preference for a more comfortable suburban life, many blacks feel guilty that they have abandoned their city. Lucenia Dunn moved from Washington to Woodmere, a predominately black development, in 1989. "We were first proud of the Chocolate City," she says, "and it's hard to unloosen that level of loyalty to the concept of having a successful African-American-owned and operated and run city. It grieves us that it's in trouble."

ETHNIC WASHINGTON, D.C.

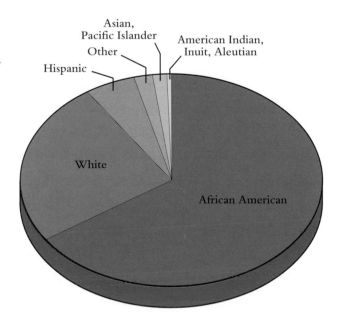

Maryland's Prince George's County has become one of the largest black suburbs in the country. Ironically, some of the county's richer African-American citizens have begun to worry about their home becoming a haven for the city's poorer blacks. As one resident noted: "People have moved here away from crime to good schools, and it's very clear that some don't want ghetto kids in their school buildings." Alvin Thorton, a school board member, agreed that "Some middle-class black people have the same prejudices as their older white counterparts." In Washington, as in many American cities, there are class divisions within different ethnic groups. In the end, only if Washington can pick itself up by the bootstraps—improve its schools, fund its police force, and fix its potholes—will blacks, rich and poor, be inclined to take another risk on the city.

LIVING TOGETHER

Since the 1980s, Washington has become home to many people of Hispanic descent. The first arrivals were mostly refugees from El Salvador, who had fled that country's harsh right-wing regimes. These newcomers settled in Mount Pleasant and Adams-Morgan, and the community grew quickly as more and more Salvadorans followed in search of greater economic opportunity.

Unfortunately, the Hispanics weren't greeted with open arms by the black community. In the early 1990s, there were a series of riots in Mount Pleasant between Hispanic and black young men. In a real race-reversal, some Hispanics accused black policemen of discrimination. Though there undoubtedly remain some ill feelings, the tensions have decreased notably in recent years.

Children enjoy the playground at an Hispanic festival.

Washington is also full of well-off people who are committed to living in the nation's capital, people who thrive on the pace, grit, and excitement that goes with living in an international city. The wealthiest, many of whose families have been in the district for generations, generally live in the Spring Valley area, often on Foxhill Road, in the upper Northwest section of the city. Most other middle- to upper-class people of all races have moved to the district to work for the federal government. Very well educated (there are more Ph.D.s per person in Washington than anywhere else in the

A car burns in the Mount Pleasant riots.

world), this group, sometimes described as "government wonks," don't usually settle in the district for good.

Many Washingtonians are loyal to their city and are making an effort to bridge the racial divide. As one resident put it: "I don't think there are black, white, or Hispanic potholes." There are people of all walks of life who take time out of their day to help the less fortunate. In Ward 8, the Arthur Ashe Foundation provides tennis lessons for inner-city children. Despite limited funds, the Children of Mine, an organization founded by a woman named Hannah M. Hawkins, provides after-school meals, tutoring, and counseling to poor children. Another involved Wash-

RECIPE: SENATE BEAN SOUP

The story goes that Fred Thomas Dubois, a senator from Idaho from 1901 to 1907, was such a bean soup fan that he forced a resolution through Congress requiring that it be on the Senate lunch menu every day. Other people give Senator Kunte Nelson of Minnesota the credit for introducing bean soup to the Congressional kitchen in 1903. Regardless of who introduced it, Senate Bean Soup is the hottest-selling dish in town. In fact, it is so popular that the Senate dining room makes it in fifty gallon batches . . . three times a week! Have an adult help you with this recipe.

    2 pounds small navy beans
    1½ pounds smoked ham hocks
    1 onion
    butter
    salt and pepper

Wash the beans in hot water until they are white. Put beans in 4 quarts of hot water. Add the ham hocks and boil slowly for approximately three hours in a covered pot.

Chop the onion and braise in butter. When the onion is a little brown add to the soup. Season with salt and pepper.

John Trumbull memorialized the signing of the Declaration of Independence in his painting, which hangs in the Capitol.

ingtonian, Melissa Kunstader, who fought successfully to keep all of Washington's twenty-seven library branches open, says: "I wish D.C. could get over this racial nonsense. There is quite a bit of elbow room to bring people together in this city."

THE ARTS

One problem Washington definitely does not have is a lack of things to do. Among the city's great strengths are its museums, monuments, parks, and historic sights. And that doesn't include its varied neighborhoods, its art, or its restaurants.

Many Washingtonians enjoy the fine art collections in their city—from the National Portrait Gallery to the Phillips Collection (a private museum of contemporary art), there is a lot to see. Washington's government buildings are also graced by much fine art. John Trumbull, an early American painter, created the beautiful *The Declaration of Independence, July 4, 1776* that hangs in the Capitol Rotunda. Also in the capital are bronzed statues of Thomas Jefferson and Benjamin Franklin. As a local fireman put it, "There's art pretty much everywhere around here. You don't have to search too hard."

There is also a thriving music scene in the district. The National Symphony Orchestra, which was founded in 1931, plays regularly at the John F. Kennedy Concert Hall. Then there's the marine band—a special Washington treat. Founded in 1798 by an act of Congress, this band has performed at every presidential inauguration since 1801. The group's most famous leader was John Philip Sousa, the king of march music, who composed such favorites as "The Stars and Stripes Forever."

SPORTS

All Washingtonians have one important thing in common: an adoration for the Washington Redskins that borders on insanity. But there are other teams in the nation's capital as well. The Washington Bullets have recently rebuilt their basketball team with young stars and appear to be on the verge of being contenders. But Washington's

The thunderous brass of the United States Marine Band

reputation as the Murder Capital caused the Bullets to change their name. In 1997, fans began cheering the Washington Wizards instead.

Those with a taste for college basketball can follow Georgetown, which became a powerhouse under coach John Thompson and has produced such NBA stars as Patrick Ewing and Alonzo Mourning. Last but not least, Washington has a hockey team, named the Capitals. While no one could mistake the district for a hockey-crazed town like Montreal, the Capitals have a strong following.

THE REDSKINS

A tie that binds most Washingtonians together—regardless of race, religion, or wealth—is their football team, the Redskins.

One diehard fan remarked, "People here are nuts for the 'Skins.' Absolutely, certifiably nuts!"

It's true—Washingtonians have stayed loyal to their team through good times and bad. The team is so popular that divorcing couples have asked the courts to fairly divide their season tickets. Their home games have been sold out for close to thirty years, and over forty thousand people are on the waiting list for season tickets. The good news for nonfans is that Sunday afternoons in the fall are the best times to shop. "That's when I buy my week's groceries," Sheila Cribbs, a mother of three, said. "Everyone else is at the stadium or parked in front of the TV."

Indeed, the popularity of the team convinced team owner Jack Kent Cooke to build a bigger stadium, which seats seventy-eight thousand people. Although the new stadium is in Maryland, many loyal fans forgave their team for moving across the border: There are twenty-thousand more seats available per game!

Still, Washington remains a football town. "Basketball and hockey are OK," one fan said. "But time stops around here for the Redskins. Football is the one things that brings everyone in this city together."

FESTIVALS AND EVENTS

Springtime brings Washingtonians downtown to the Mall to participate in a variety of festivals. The most famous is the Cherry Blossom Festival, celebrated each April to mark the beautiful blossoms on the cherry trees at the city's Tidal Basin. But many others are also worth keeping an eye out for.

"My favorite," says second grader John True, "is the kite festival."

The Princess Float in the annual Cherry Blossom Festival Parade.

The kite festival is one of Washington's most popular spring events; one of the most colorful, too.

THE INAUGURATION

No other city can boast an event as stirring as the inauguration, a time every four years when the president is sworn in and addresses the nation. In 1933, Franklin Roosevelt told the country that was suffering from the ravages of the Great Depression, "The only thing we have to fear is fear itself." In 1961, John F. Kennedy implored the nation: "Ask not what your country can do for you: ask what you can do for your country."

The inauguration is also a time of great celebration. In 1996, a musical about Martin Luther King Jr. with lyrics by Maya Angelou was performed. Many movie stars were called upon to host special events. In fact, Whoopi Goldberg was given a special presidential convoy to ensure her timely arrival from New York. Other stars come for the atmosphere and the parties. Reportedly, President Clinton attended fourteen formal balls on the day of his second inauguration. (When President Jackson was inaugurated back in 1829, he shocked the wealthier set by inviting his less refined friends over to the White House.)

As with any party, much of the chatter is not about important world issues. Instead, it is focused on who is wearing what. In 1997, one famous actress reportedly called the Willard Hotel from her jet to say she had left her fur wrap at home and needed a new one desperately!

Japanese dancers display their talent at the Festival of American Folklife.

Spring is marked in the district each year by hundreds of techni-
color kites dipping and diving around and above the Washington
Monument. In June and early July, contributions that different
ethnic groups have made to our country are celebrated in the
Smithsonian Festival of American Folk Life. Set up on the Mall,

the festival brings together a large array of people, food, arts, crafts, and exhibits. Though not technically a festival, the National Symphony Open Air Concerts give all Washingtonians a reason to take a picnic and blanket to the Capitol grounds and listen to beautiful music. A special treat is on July 4 when fireworks shoot up over the Washington Monument as the orchestra plays.

"And the rockets red glare! The bombs bursting in air!" Fourth of July fireworks by the Capitol

5 WASHINGTON'S BEST

African Americans celebrate black pride in the Million Man March.

At one time or another, the District of Columbia has been home to virtually every important politician in America. But throughout the years, a few well-known Americans have put their own personal stamp on the nation's capital.

THE FOUNDING FATHER

It is ironic that the man who gave his name to his country's capital never actually lived there. When George Washington became president in 1789, New York was the nation's capital, and he and the first lady, Martha, lived in what is now lower Manhattan. That August they followed the federal government to Philadelphia.

But even though Washington never actually lived in the city that bears his name, he did have a lot to do with what it eventually looked like. Assigned the task of choosing a capital in 1790, he opted for a spot close to his Mount Vernon, Virginia, home. His reputation throughout the country as general and president enabled him to hire Pierre L'Enfant to build the city as he wanted.

But Washington's influence on the city goes deeper than that. It was the honor with which George Washington carried himself as the first president that gave America's new government legitimacy. Without his sure hand overseeing the infant republic, America may not have survived and then thrived. After all, America was attempting

George Washington at Mount Vernon, *by George Hicks. The father of our country has lent his famous name to one nation's capital, one state, thirty-one counties, and twenty-two cities and towns.*

something never before accomplished: the establishment of a democracy on a massive scale. George Washington was the steady, firm leader to whom all could turn. When he wanted to step down from the presidency after his first term in office, two bitter rivals, Thomas Jefferson, then secretary of state, and Alexander Hamilton, the secretary of the treasury, begged him to remain. By the time he did retire in 1797, he had successfully guided America through a rocky start. The experimental stage of the country was over, and the presidency could be turned over to someone else.

A POET FOR THE NATION

One of America's most notable poets, Walt Whitman, lived a good portion of his life in the nation's capital. Born in 1819 in New York,

"I am the poet of the Body and I am the poet of the Soul,
The pleasures of heaven are with me and the pains of hell are with me."
—Walt Whitman, from "Song of Myself"

O CAPTAIN! MY CAPTAIN!

When President Abraham Lincoln was assassinated on April 14, 1865, Walt Whitman gave words to the country's enormous grief in his poem "O Captain! My Captain!" which ends:

My Captain does not answer, his lips are pale and still,
My father does not feel my arm, he has no pulse or will,
The ship is anchor'd safe and sound, its voyage closed and done,
From fearful trip the victor ship comes in with object won;
Exult O shores, and ring O bells!
But I with mournful tread,
Walk the deck my Captain lies,
Fallen cold and dead.

Painting by
George Peter Alexander Healy, 1887

Whitman spent his twenties writing editorials for the *Daily Eagle*, proving himself a diehard abolitionist (someone who opposed slavery). Several years after winning acclaim with his first book of poems, *Leaves of Grass*, published in 1855, Whitman, a true humanitarian, moved to Washington, D.C., to help care for stricken troops during the Civil War. "The hurt and wounded I pacify with soothing hand," he wrote in 1862. "I sit by the restless all the dark night. Some are so young!" When President Lincoln was assassinated in 1865, the poet expressed the country's grief in "When Lilacs Last in the Dooryard Bloom'd" and "O Captain! My Captain!"

After the Civil War, Whitman was given a clerkship in the Department of the Interior but was dismissed when his superior discovered a copy of *Leaves of Grass* and thought it "an indecent book," probably because of sexual references. Whitman soon landed another job in the attorney general's office, but an illness forced him to leave Washington. He spent the years until his death in 1892 in New Jersey and England. Though he didn't spend all of his life in Washington, it is the city that perhaps remembers him best.

THE WRY OBSERVER

Washington, D.C., is populated by some pretty self-important men and women. Luckily, there are journalists like Russell Baker to shake them up a bit and bring them back to earth.

Born in rural Virginia in 1925, Baker was raised by a mother who insisted that he "make something" of himself. He was hired by the *Baltimore Sun* in 1947 and later moved to the *New York Times*.

Russell Baker, wry commentator on life inside the Beltway

When he was given a biweekly "Observer" column in 1962, Baker's reputation as a humorous commentator on the foibles of government grew quickly.

Wise as well as witty, Baker has poked fun at presidents, senators, and justices for three and a half decades. His humor often comes laced with common sense. "Cultivate luck," he once wrote. "For without it greatness is beyond reach. What would Franklin

Roosevelt's reputation be today if the Nazis had made the atomic bomb first? Suppose Lincoln's and James K. Polk's places in the order of Presidents had been reversed. Washington today might have a magnificent Polk Memorial, and adults might ask: 'Who the hell was Abraham Lincoln?'"

Russell Baker was awarded the Pulitzer Prize for Distinguished Commentary and the George Polk Award for Commentary in 1979. But awards haven't slowed him down. Baker gleefully continues to poke fun at the power elite in the nation's capital twice a week in the *New York Times*.

Elegant jazzman Duke Ellington at the piano in the 1920s

MAKING MUSIC

One of the most influential jazz composers and orchestra leaders of his day, Duke Ellington was born in Washington in 1899, the son of a butler. By 1918, he was leading a band in the district. Soon, Ellington was touring the country with his own jazz orchestra for which he wrote all the compositions and arrangements. Ellington became known for such standards as "Satin Doll," "Mood Indigo," and "Take the A Train." Though he was spurned for a Pulitzer Prize in music in 1965, Ellington, an urbane man of sixty-six, took the rejection in stride, saying: "Fate doesn't want me to be too famous too young."

Ellington died in 1974 and is remembered as one of pop music's most original artists and certainly the greatest musical talent our nation's capital has produced.

THE BIG TRAIN

Washington has had many sports heroes throughout its history, but none can compare to Walter Johnson, the great pitcher for the Washington Senators from 1907 to 1927. Nicknamed the Big Train in honor of his thunderous fastball, Johnson was one of the first five players elected to the Baseball Hall of Fame (in 1936, along with Ty Cobb, Babe Ruth, Honus Wagner, and Christy Mathewson).

Back in those days, pitchers got to the mound more often. Over one long weekend in 1908, Johnson started three times . . . and won all three games in shutouts! When facing the strikeout king, opposing batters used to mutter, "How can you hit them if you

Washington's first great athlete, Walter Johnson of the Senators

can't see them?" as they watched his pitches whiz by. In his twenty-one-year career with the Senators, Johnson struck out 3,508 batters and won 416 games, 114 by shutouts.

Unfortunately, Johnson's teams (like some of the city's teams today) were seldom very good. After years of losing records, the Senators finally won the World Series in 1924. Johnson, then thirty-seven years old, won the deciding seventh game. Fans every-where agreed that no one deserved it more. The Big Train was also notoriously big-hearted, a great athlete and a gentle man. He may not be a household name anymore, but Walter Johnson's spirit still pervades the sports arenas of the nation's capital.

6 A MONUMENT TO OUR HISTORY

Washington, D.C., is a tourist's dream. Nowhere else in America is our country's heritage, its magnificence and tragedy, so gloriously on display. Though spring is the most beautiful time of year, the district is a thrilling place to visit during every season.

A WALK ALONG THE MALL

As one Washingtonian said: "The Mall has it all." Indeed, there are so many monuments, statues, and museums along this famous strip that it is impossible to do justice to them all. Here is a sample of some of the most interesting spots that you won't want to miss.

The Lincoln Memorial. At the head of the reflecting pool stands the famous memorial to Abraham Lincoln, the nation's sixteenth president, who led America safely through the Civil War. Soon after his assassination in 1865, a memorial was planned to honor his memory, but it was not until 1912 that the current site was chosen by Congress. Henry Bacon was selected to design the marble building, and the first cornerstone was laid on the anniversary of Lincoln's birthday in 1915.

Sculpted by Daniel Chester French, the centerpiece of the memorial is a nineteen-foot statue of Lincoln sitting thoughtfully on a chair. To the left, the words to the Gettysburg Address,

PLACES TO SEE

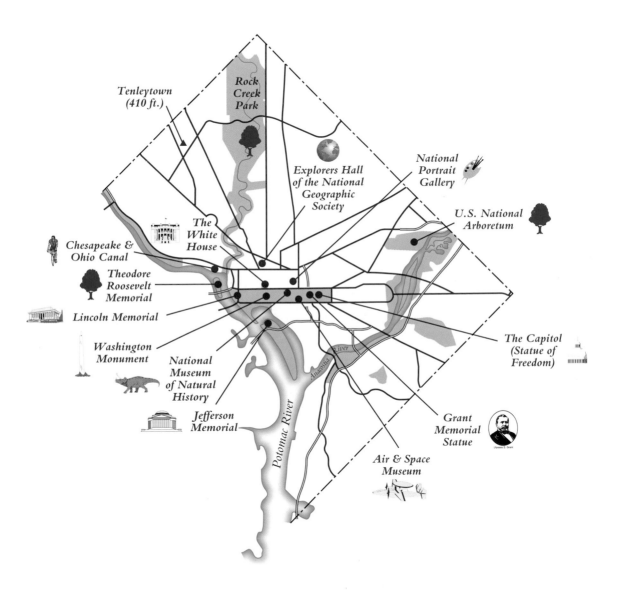

Tenleytown
(410 ft.)

Rock
Creek
Park

Explorers Hall
of the National
Geographic
Society

National
Portrait
Gallery

U.S. National
Arboretum

The
White
House

Chesapeake &
Ohio Canal

Theodore
Roosevelt
Memorial

Lincoln Memorial

Washington
Monument

National
Museum
of Natural
History

Jefferson
Memorial

Potomac River

Anacostia River

The Capitol
(Statue of
Freedom)

Grant
Memorial
Statue

Ulysses S. Grant

Air & Space
Museum

delivered by Lincoln to the Northern troops near the end of the Civil War, are carved into the wall. On a mural above the address the Angel of Truth frees a slave. To the right of Lincoln's statue are the words to his second inaugural address, delivered in the waning moments of the Civil War, in which he urged his countrymen, "With malice toward none, with charity for all, . . . to do all which may achieve and cherish a just and lasting peace among ourselves and with all nations."

Through the years, the Lincoln Memorial has been the site of many important historical events. Most notably, in 1963 Martin Luther King Jr. delivered his famous "I have a dream" speech from the steps of the monument.

The Vietnam Veterans Memorial. From the Revolutionary War to the Korean War, the American public always believed in the causes for which they were asked to fight. The Vietnam War marked the first time that a large portion of Americans felt we were in the wrong. During the late 1960s, some young people burned their draft cards and marched for peace, and many political leaders spoke out against U.S. involvement in the conflict.

By the war's end in 1975, fifty-eight thousand Americans had died in Vietnam. A twenty-one-year-old Yale University student, Maya Ying Lin, created the design to honor these men and women. She decided that "The names would become the memorial." Although the Vietnam Veterans Memorial is simple—a series

The Vietnam Veterans Memorial is one of Washington's most popular and moving sites.

of black marble slabs with the name of every single soldier who died in the war carved in the stone in small white letters—it conveys great emotion. Known now to many simply as the Wall, this deeply affecting memorial has become one of Washington's most popular since it opened in 1982.

The Washington Monument. Past the reflecting pool, the district's most famous landmark stands 555 feet high. First suggested in 1783 (the founding fathers' original idea was a simple statue of General Washington on his horse), the monument did not actually begin to take shape until 1848. The Civil War halted construction, and later, work stopped again for lack of funds. (About 150 feet up the side of the memorial, it's easy to see where work was stopped by the slight difference in the color of the marble.) The monument was finally completed and opened to the public in 1888.

The Washington Monument is the tallest masonry structure in the world. Views from the top are extraordinary, but the lines can be long!

The Jefferson Memorial. Thomas Jefferson was the author of the Declaration of Independence, secretary of state under George Washington, and our nation's third president. Though he died on July 4, 1826, exactly fifty years to the day after the signing of his famous declaration, a memorial in his honor was not completed until April 13, 1943. Jefferson was also an architect with a fondness for domed structures (like his home in Monticello, Virginia), and his memorial is appropriately enough built in the same style. On the inside of the monument words to some of Jefferson's most famous speeches are engraved in the walls. Smack in the center of

Engraved on the walls of the Jefferson Memorial are Jefferson's words: "I have sworn upon the altar of God eternal hostility against every form of tyranny over the mind of man."

the dome is a nineteen-foot-tall bronze figure of Jefferson, wearing a long fur-lined coat, knee pants, and buckled shoes.

The Jefferson Memorial is widely regarded as one of the prettiest spots in the city. "The view across the Tidal Basin to downtown Washington is gorgeous," John Crimmons, a longtime resident, says, "especially in the spring when the cherry blossoms are in bloom. It's one of my favorite places on the planet."

THE NATIONAL ARCHIVES

We hold these truths to be self-evident, that all men are created equal, that they are endowed by their Creator with certain unalienable Rights, that among these are Life, Liberty, and the pursuit of Happiness.
—Thomas Jefferson, the Declaration of Independence

Virtually no American child grows up without studying the Declaration of Independence, the Constitution, and the Bill of Rights, perhaps the three most important documents in our nation's history.

The original copies of these documents are kept under glass at the National Archives. There you can see Thomas Jefferson's famous

THE SMITHSONIAN MUSEUMS

Take a walk along the Mall and you are likely to see some interesting looking buildings. Is that a Greek temple? Or a medieval castle? Actually, these buildings are part of perhaps the most impressive string of museums in the country, if not the world. The Smithsonian

pronouncement to the world of America's decision to fight for its freedom from the British. At the bottom is John Hancock's famous signature!

Pages one and four of the Constitution are also on display, along with the signatures of the delegates to the Constitutional Convention in 1787. The Bill of Rights, which sets forth freedom of the press, speech, and worship is also exhibited.

To keep these precious documents safe, the glass case is lowered twenty feet each evening into a specially designed bomb-proof vault!

d States, in order to form a more perfect Union, establish Justice,
the general Welfare, and secure the Blessings of Liberty to ourselves
the States of America.

Institution was established in 1846 by an English scientist named James Smithson, who donated a large sum of money to the United States government to found an organization devoted to increasing knowledge. Today, Smithson's bequest has been turned into a series of

The "castle" at the Smithsonian Museum

fascinating museums that every family member can enjoy. "And what is great," says Barbara Eyman, a Washington lawyer, "is that they are free!"

Again, there's not enough room to list them all, but here are a few you won't want to miss.

The National Air and Space Museum. Have you ever wondered what the Wright brothers first airplane looked like? Well, it's on display here, along with the *Spirit of St. Louis*, the plane that Charles Lindbergh piloted on the first nonstop solo trip across the Atlantic Ocean on May 20-21, 1927. (It took him more than thirty-three hours, considered fast traveling in those days).

The museum also holds the *Friendship 7* space capsule, the first ship to orbit the earth, and *Skylab*, the first space station, as well as a genuine moon rock. Also thrilling are the IMAX films, about space and air travel, shown on screens so large you get the feeling that you are flying yourself.

The National Museum of American History. Perhaps the

The National Air and Space Museum displays planes from throughout the history of flight.

first thing you'll notice in the front entrance of this museum is the Foucault Pendulum that swings slowly back and forth, never stopping. Each time it knocks down one of the red markers that surround it in a circle, it gives proof that the earth is rotating.

But this museum is mainly devoted to collecting odd artifacts of American history. Everything is here—from the ruby slippers Dorothy wore in *The Wizard of Oz* to a display of gowns worn by our nation's first ladies. Perhaps best of all is the floor devoted to automobiles—everything from the earliest Model T to the fanciest sports car. There are also old bicycles, trains, and rooms of model ships.

The National Museum of Natural History. "I looked up and there it was. An absolutely giant elephant. Very cool," said Brenda Childs, a fifth grader from Arlington, Virginia. Indeed, a single step into the Natural History Museum gets you into the swing of things. Standing in the main lobby is a thirteen-foot-tall, eight-ton African bush elephant.

And there's more inside—81 million artifacts documenting humankind and the natural environment—everything from reassembled dinosaur skeletons to the 45.5-carat Hope Diamond, one of the largest jewels in the world. Also exciting is the newly remodeled O. Orkin Insect Zoo, which includes displays on the evolution of insects and a giant collection of bugs. Children can crawl through a fourteen-foot model of an African termite house, and there is a giant beehive (safely behind glass), not to mention live cockroaches and leaf-cutter ants. "It's one of my favorite places to take the kids," says Rachel Hill, a Washington mother. "I've just got to make sure they don't bring any of the live exhibits home!"

This African Bush Elephant guards the entrance of the Natural History Museum.

THE WHITE HOUSE

It's an odd fact that the only president who did not live in the White House was George Washington. The reason? It wasn't built. When John Adams moved in in the year 1800, it was hardly the beautiful mansion it is today. The War of 1812 didn't help, either,

THE CHERRY BLOSSOM FESTIVAL

Perhaps Washington's most beautiful sight is the annual blooming of its cherry trees. The lovely trees were donated to the United States as a friendship gift by the mayor of Tokyo in 1912 to mark the "ephemeral nature of beauty." They bloom for about two weeks every spring.

The Cherry Festival Parade is usually slated for the first Saturday in April. But as one longtime D.C. resident put it: "Depending on Mother Nature the blossoms are sometimes either not out yet or already gone!" As a result, parties and ceremonies in honor of the cherry blossoms run from late March through early April.

Tourists flood the city in these weeks. During a special ceremony, a three-hundred-year-old Japanese lantern is lit. This is followed by a speech on friendship by the Japanese ambassador and talks by representatives of the U.S. government.

Smart blossom-peepers use the Metro to get downtown to avoid the agony of parking. And some tourists head to the Maryland suburbs, notably Kenwood, which has beautiful cherry blossoms of its own but no crowds.

This mansion is available for rent every four years. The price? The willingness to lead the country.

when the mansion was severely burned by the British. It took several years of work before it was once again ready for occupation in 1817. As years have passed, the presidential mansion has been improved. In 1833, running water was added. Gaslights replaced oil lamps in 1849. Though historians are unsure, Millard Fillmore is credited with installing the first bathtub in 1851. No one disputes the fact that our twenty-seventh president, 340-pound William Howard Taft, had a custom-made tub installed that was large enough for four grown men.

The White House has 132 rooms—some of them famous, such as Lincoln's bedroom. Perhaps the most important is the Oval Office, where the president works. Much of the government's important business still takes place in the White House.

THE HOLOCAUST MEMORIAL MUSEUM

One of the district's most powerful sites, the Holocaust Memorial Museum tells the story of the six million Jews and others who were killed by the Nazis between 1933 and 1945. Documenting the horrors of the Holocaust through photos, film, artifacts, and inter-active exhibits, this museum is best viewed with a parent or school group. In one exhibit, "Daniel's Story: Remember the Children," you follow the life of Daniel and his family, walking through rooms that show his home before the Nazis took power and learning how this boy was affected by the Holocaust. Open only since 1993, the Holocaust Memorial Museum is one of the finest new additions to the city.

NATURE IN WASHINGTON

Washington is a city with plenty of places to go for a little dose of nature. "The arboretum is so still and quiet," says Mary Neuwirth, an architect. "I go there to walk and unwind." With 444 acres of

The Holocaust Memorial Museum reminds visitors of the individual lives led by the millions killed by the Nazis.

trees, flowers, and plants, the National Arboretum is a great place to relax and forget about the pressures of school or work. Like many areas in Washington, it is especially beautiful in the spring, when covered by azaleas. The rhododendrons in the summer are lovely as well.

Smack in the middle of the city is Rock Creek Park, which covers nearly two thousand acres of rolling hills, woods, and meadows. Although Rock Creek has over fifteen miles of trails, you don't have to take a long hike to enjoy the park. Many Washingtonians use it in the course of a normal business day. "It's great to be able to walk to work on a nice day through Rock Creek," says Frank Clines. "It's one of the things I really appreciate about living in this city."

Rock Creek Park is especially nice on weekends when its roads are closed to cars and joggers, and bikers and roller-bladers take over.

This survey of Washington's sites is by no means complete. There is the Library of Congress, the National Gallery of Art, the Navy Museum, the Hirshhorn Museum and Sculpture Garden, the National Museum of American Art, the National Portrait Gallery, the National Postal Museum. . . . The list is endless. Come for a weekend and start looking. Or you can take the advice of Jeffrey Livingston, a D.C. security guard, who said, "It takes weeks to see everything here. If you really want to see it all, you've got to move here."

Picnickers on the bank of the Potomac

STARS & BARS: The Stars and Bars is the official communications symbol of the District of Columbia

THE FLAG: Three red stars float above two red stripes against a white background on the District of Columbia flag. The design is based on George Washington's family coat of arms and was adopted in 1938.

THE SEAL: A woman who represents Justice places a wreath on a statue of George Washington. The national bird, a bald eagle, sits next to Justice. In the background, the Capitol appears on the right, and the sun, proclaiming a new day, rises on the left. The seal was adopted in 1871.

DISTRICT SURVEY

Established: President George Washington chose the site of the city in 1790. It became the nation's capital on December 1, 1800.

Origin of Name: Washington is named for the nation's first president, George Washington. The District of Columbia is named for explorer Christopher Columbus.

Nickname: The Nation's Capital

Motto: Justice for All

Bird: Wood thrush

Flower: American beauty rose

Tree: Scarlet oak

Rose

Wood thrush

WE SHALL OVERCOME

This simple yet moving hymn was the theme song of the civil rights movement of the 1960s. The hymn's roots are an old black church song, "I'll Overcome Some Day". It has been sung at mass rallies by thousands of voices and has echoed around the world in many languages. On August 28, 1963, over 200,000 people gathered on the Mall in Washington, D.C., to hear Martin Luther King Jr. deliver his famous "I have a dream" speech and to sing "We Shall Overcome."

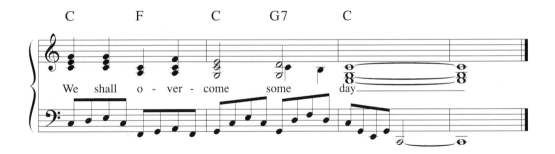

We are not afraid,
We are not afraid,
We are not afraid today,
Oh, deep in my heart, I do believe,
We shall overcome some day.

We are not alone . . . (today) . . .
The truth shall make us free . . . (some day) . . .
We'll walk hand in hand . . . (today) . . .
The Lord will see us through . . . (today) . . .
Repeat first verse

GEOGRAPHY

Highest Point: 410 feet above sea level at Tenleytown

Lowest Point: Sea level at the Potomac River

Area: 68.25 square miles

Greatest Distance, North to South: 15 miles

Greatest Distance, East to West: 14 miles

Bordering States: Maryland to the northwest, northeast, and southeast; Virginia to the southwest

Average January Temperature: 35° F

Average July Temperature: 78.9° F

Hottest Recorded Temperature: 106° F on July 20, 1930

Coldest Recorded Temperature: −15° F on February 11, 1899

Average Annual Precipitation: 50 inches

Major Rivers: Anacostia, Potomac

Bodies of Water: Tidal Basin of the Potomac River, Washington Channel

Trees: beech, black walnut, cedar of Lebanon, dogwood, elm, holly, linden, locust, Lombardy poplar, magnolia, maple, oriental plane, pine, pin oak, red oak, scarlet oak, spreading ginkgo, sycamore, willow

Wild Plants: bloodroot, cattail, hepatica, iris, jack-in-the-pulpit, pickerelweed, skunk cabbage, trailing arbutus, Virginia bluebell, water hyacinth

Animals: chipmunk, fox, frog, muskrat, opossum, rabbit, raccoon, squirrel, turtle, woodchuck

Raccoon

Birds: Baltimore oriole, blue jay, chickadee, duck, heron, finch, mockingbird, pigeon, sparrow, starling, thrush, warbler, woodpecker

Fish: catfish, largemouth bass, pickerel, shad, striped bass, sunfish, walleyed pike

Endangered Animals: American peregrine falcon, bald eagle, Hays Spring amphipod

Bald Eagle

TIMELINE

Washington, D.C., History

c. 1600 Piscataway Indians live near the Potomac and Anacostia rivers in present-day Washington, D.C.

1634 English settlers, led by Leonard Calvert, build the first town along the Potomac River

1751 City of Georgetown is established

1776 The Declaration of Independence is signed on July 4

1789 George Washington becomes the first president of the United States

1791 Virginia and Maryland cede land for the creation of a federal district; George Washington chooses Pierre L'Enfant, a French engineer, to design the nation's capital city

1793 George Washington lays the cornerstone for the U. S. Capitol building

1800 President John Adams and his family move into the White House

1814 Admiral Sir George Cockburn orders British forces to burn the White House during the War of 1812; while rebuilding, the exterior walls are painted white to cover the fire damage, which results in the building being called the White House

1847 Congress returns to Virginia ceded land that is unnecessary for federal government use

1848 Construction of the Washington Monument begins

1857 Gallaudet College opens, offering collegiate courses to the deaf

1861 Troops from New York's Seventh Regiment protect Washington, D.C., from the advancing Confederates during the Civil War

1865 Abraham Lincoln is assassinated by John Wilkes Booth at Ford's Theatre

1867 Howard University is founded as an "institution of higher learning for Negroes"

1874 Congress passes legislation taking away the right to vote from D.C. citizens

1888 Washington Monument opens to the public

1901 Theodore Roosevelt prints the words "The White House" on his presidential stationery, making the name official

1912 Japan sends a gift of 3,000 flowering cherry trees to the United States to be planted in the nation's capital

1919 In anti-Negro riots, mobs kill 4 African Americans and wound 70

1922 Lincoln Memorial is completed

1943 Jefferson Memorial opens

1944 Senator Theodore Bilbo proposes legislation to deport black D.C. citizens to Africa

1963 Martin Luther King Jr. delivers "I have a dream" speech

1964 Twenty-third Amendment to the Constitution grants District of Columbia citizens the right to vote in presidential elections

1968 Riots break out in response to the assassination of Martin Luther King Jr.

c. 1970 Potomac River cleanup effort is successful, allowing fish to survive in the river

1970 District of Columbia voters allowed to elect a nonvoting delegate to the House of Representatives

1973 Home rule instituted, enabling District of Columbia voters to elect their own mayor and city council

1978 Marion Barry is elected mayor of the District of Columbia

1990 Sharon Pratt Kelly becomes the first female mayor of Washington

CALENDAR OF CELEBRATIONS

Presidential Inauguration Although this January event occurs only once every four years, it is a major celebration in the city. The newly elected president parades down Pennsylvania Avenue from the U.S. Capitol building to the steps of the White House to take the oath of office. A festive parade with floats, bands from each state, and marching military units passes by the president's reviewing stand.

Black History Month February is the month when Washington, D.C., and all America pay tribute to the forward-thinking and courageous African Americans who have contributed so much to this country. Special events are held at the Smithsonian Institution and the Martin Luther King Jr., Library.

Abraham Lincoln's Birthday February 12 marks the birthday of the 16th president. At exactly noon, a reading of the Gettysburg Address booms forth from the Lincoln Memorial

George Washington's Birthday The city that bears his name honors the first president with a parade in late February.

Cherry Blossom Festival A two-week-long festival marks the blossoming of the cherry trees along the Potomac River. This annual event commemorates the 3,000 cherry trees given to America by Japan in 1912 to bond the two countries' friendship. The highlight of the celebration is the Cherry Festival Parade, which is usually held on the first Saturday in April.

Sakura Matsuri This annual April festival honors Japanese-American relations. It features artists, martial arts demonstrations, authentic Japanese cuisine, ikebana (flower-arranging) workshops, and children's activities, including origami and wood carving.

White House Easter Egg Roll On the Monday after Easter Sunday, people flock to the grounds of the Ellipse, the park behind the White House, where 1,000 wooden eggs are hidden. Entertainers, food, and contests enliven the day. Adults must be accompanied by a child or they are not admitted.

White House Easter Egg Roll

Smithsonian Kite Festival Every spring kite fliers gather at the Mall near the Washington Monument to enjoy a day of spectacular kite flying. Hundreds of colorful kites whip and wave around the monument.

Memorial Day Weekend This three-day event includes parades, wreath-laying ceremonies at the Tomb of the Unknown Soldier (across the Potomac in Arlington, Virginia), and the annual National Memorial Day Concert by the National Symphony on the west lawn of the U.S. Capitol.

Festival of American Folklife See, hear, smell, taste, and look at the display of arts and crafts created by representatives of American regional and ethnic cultures at this lively weeklong event sponsored by the Smithsonian Institution. Songs, music, and dancing add to the entertainment every June on the Mall.

Independence Day The Fourth of July is a very special celebration in Washington, D.C. The day begins with a parade down Constitution Avenue, which is followed by entertainment and concerts all through the day and evening. The grand finale is a spectacular fireworks display above the Washington Monument.

D.C. Blues Festival The finest blues singers and bands perform in Anacostia

Park each summer at this free festival. Headliners include nationally known figures such as Smokey Wilson and the local D.C. Blues Society Band.

Adams-Morgan Day On the first Sunday after Labor Day the residents of this multiethnic neighborhood hold a fair with dancing, music, food, and arts and crafts from Africa, Latin America, and the Caribbean.

National Christmas Tree Lighting The lighting of the National Christmas Tree by the president is part of the seasonal Pageant of Peace. Nightly musical programs cascade across the grounds of the Ellipse throughout the holiday season.

Edward Albee

DISTRICT STARS

Edward Albee (1928–   ) is a playwright who was born in Washington, D.C. His best-known work, *Who's Afraid of Virginia Woolf?* was made into a popular movie starring Elizabeth Taylor and Richard Burton. Albee has won the Pulitzer Prize three times for his plays, *A Delicate Balance, Three Tall Women*, and *Seascape*.

Marion Barry (1936–   ), who was born in Memphis, Tennessee, has long been active in Washington, D.C. He came to prominence for his work in downtown renewal during the 1970s. Barry was first elected mayor in 1978. He was reelected twice, but then in the late 1980s, he was convicted of drug possession. Even after serving a prison sentence, he remained popular and was again elected mayor.

Clara Barton (1821–1912) became known as the Angel of the Battlefield for her work tending the wounded in Washington, D.C., during the Civil War. After the war she helped organize the American Red Cross, which provides aid in times of war and natural disaster.

Elgin Baylor (1934–   ) was one of basketball's great forwards. Born in Washington, D.C., he played for the Minneapolis and Los Angeles Lakers.

Alexander Graham Bell (1847–1922), who moved to Washington, D.C., in 1879, is best remembered for inventing the telephone. A man of many talents, he had a lifelong interest in helping the deaf and hard of hearing. From 1896 to 1904 he was president of the Washington-based National Geographic Society.

Frances Hodgson Burnett (1849–1924) built a house in Washington, D.C., with proceeds from her successful book and play *Little Lord Fauntleroy*. Today she is best known for her book *The Secret Garden*, which has been adapted for stage and film.

Connie Chung (1946–   ) is a Washington-born journalist. She has anchored several television news shows including *News at Sunrise* and *Saturday Night with Connie Chung*.

John Foster Dulles (1888–1959) was secretary of state during the administration of President Dwight D. Eisenhower. It has been said that this position was in his blood: his grandfather John W. Foster and his uncle Robert Lansing had both served as secretaries of state. Dulles was born in Washington, D.C.

Edward Kennedy "Duke" Ellington (1899–1974), the Washington-born "jazzman extraordinaire," was a pianist, orchestra leader, and composer.

Ellington left a legacy of popular songs such as "Mood Indigo," as well as longer concert works.

Katherine Graham (1917–   ) became publisher of the *Washington Post* newspaper in 1969. She championed aggressive investigative reporting of the sort made famous by reporters Carl Bernstein and Robert Woodward, who broke the story of the Watergate scandal during President Richard Nixon's term in office. They earned a Pulitzer Prize for the *Post*.

President and Mrs. Reagan with Graham

Goldie Hawn (1945–   ) was born in Washington, D.C., and attended American University before she giggled her way to stardom on television's *Laugh-In*. She won an Academy Award in 1969 for Best Supporting Actress in *Cactus Flower* and went on to star in such films as *Private Benjamin* and *The First Wives Club*.

Helen Hayes (1900–1993) was an actress known as the First Lady of the American Theatre, although she was also popular on screen, radio, and television. She won her first Academy Award in 1931 and landed another Oscar for *Airport* in 1970. The Helen Hayes Award for artistic achievement in professional theater has been established in her hometown of Washington, D.C.

Helen Hayes

J. Edgar Hoover

J. Edgar Hoover (1895–1972) was a lawyer and criminologist who served as the director of the Federal Bureau of Investigation. During 48 years of service, he is credited with turning the FBI into a fully professional organization. Hoover was born in Washington, D.C.

William Hurt (1950–   ) is an actor who won an Oscar in 1985 for his role in *The Kiss of the Spider Woman*. His many film credits include *The Big Chill* and *Children of a Lesser God*. The son of a career diplomat, Hurt was born in Washington, D.C.

Noor al-Hussein, Queen of Jordan (1951–   ) was born Lisa Najeeb Halaby in Washington, D.C. She went to school in the United States and graduated from Princeton University in 1974. In 1978, she married King Hussein of Jordan. As queen of Jordan, she directs projects on education, government, women's development, environmental protection, social welfare, and international understanding.

Queen of Jordan

Walter Johnson (1887–1946) was one of baseball's greatest pitchers. Although he was born in Kansas, he played for the Washington Senators from 1907 to 1927. Nicknamed the Big Train because of the speed of his pitching, Johnson was one of the five original inductees into the Baseball Hall of Fame.

Francis Scott Key (1779–1843) wrote the words to the national anthem, "The Star-Spangled Banner," while watching the British bombard Fort McHenry. Though born in Baltimore, he later lived in Washington, D.C., where he served as district attorney from 1833 to 1841. His house is a famous landmark in the city.

Toni Morrison (1931–   ), the author of many books including *Song of Solomon*, was born in Ohio and came to Washington, D.C., to attend Howard University. After graduation, she taught at Howard and joined a local writers' group. Morrison has received every major literary award, including the Nobel Prize for literature.

Toni Morrison

Roger Mudd (1928–   ) has worked as a reporter and newscaster for CBS and NBC. Mudd is respected for his knowledge of political affairs in his hometown of Washington, D.C.

Eleanor Holmes Norton (1937–   ) was born in the District of Columbia and has lived there most of her life. She is a lawyer who has specialized in cases involving human rights and freedom of speech. Norton formed the National Black Feminist Organization and has taught at Georgetown University School of Law. A long-time member of the House of Representatives, she is the first African-American congresswoman for the District of Columbia.

Chita Rivera (1933–   ) was born Dolores Conchita Figuero del Rivero in Washington, D.C. A popular dancer and actress, she has starred in

Broadway musicals such as *West Side Story* and *Bye, Bye, Birdie*. In 1984, she won a Tony for her role in *The Rink*.

Leonard Rose (1918–1984), born in Washington, D.C., started studying the cello at age 10. He played with the Cleveland and New York City symphony orchestras from 1938 until 1951. He has taught cello at two of the leading music schools in the country—Julliard School of Music in New York and Curtis Institute of Music in Philadelphia. Concert cellist Yo Yo Ma is one of his most successful and acclaimed students.

John Philip Sousa (1854–1932) was a Washington-born composer and musician who, in 1880, became bandmaster for the United States Marine Band. Known as the March King, Sousa went on to form his own celebrated band. He wrote comic operas, songs, suites, and more than 100 marches including "Stars and Stripes Forever" and "Semper Fidelis."

John Philip Sousa

Walt Whitman (1819–1892) was one of America's most celebrated poets. He was born in New York but spent much of his adult life in Washington, D.C. His best-known works include a volume of poetry, *Leaves of Grass*, and "O Captain! My Captain!" a poem that mourns Abraham Lincoln's death.

TOUR THE DISTRICT

The White House All the presidents of the United States except George Washington have lived in the White House. The grand mansion, its cornerstone laid in 1792, is the oldest public building in Washington, D.C. More than one million visitors tour the White House each year. The president's office and private living quarters are not open to public view.

The U.S. Capitol Building Congress conducts its business in this huge, domed building. Several architects and designers—beginning with William Thornton and including Henry Latrobe, Charles Bulfinch, E. S. Hallet, and James Hoban—developed and built the U. S. Capitol. The building's 10-ton bronze main doors portray highlights of the life of Christopher Columbus. With its majestic dome and columns, the look of the Capitol has been re-created in many statehouses across the nation.

Washington Monument Built in honor of the nation's first president, George Washington, this 555-foot white marble obelisk is circled with flags of each state of the nation. An elevator takes visitors to the top for a panoramic view of the city.

Lincoln Memorial The Lincoln Memorial is an inspirational structure built to honor one of America's greatest presidents. Inside is a huge statue sculpted by Daniel Chester French, which shows Abraham Lincoln sitting in a thoughtful pose. Selections of Lincoln's famous speeches, including the Gettysburg Address, are engraved in the walls.

Jefferson Memorial A majestic 19-foot bronze statue of Jefferson stands inside this domed building with columns circling it. Excerpts of speeches by Jefferson decorate its marble walls.

Vietnam Veterans Memorial Bold and moving, this memorial of black granite rises out of the ground between the Washington Monument and the Lincoln Memorial. The names of all who died in the Vietnam War are carved into its stone panels. This creative memorial was designed by a young Yale University architecture student, Maya Ying Lin. Nearby is a statue of two women and a wounded soldier by sculptor Glenna Goodacre, which honors women who served in the military during the Vietnam War.

National Archives This museum contains the great treasures of America: the Declaration of Independence, the U.S. Constitution, and the Bill of Rights. The archives also features murals depicting scenes of America's early history, historic treaties and documents, and photographs of Washington, D.C.

The Castle Red stone towers rise above this medieval-style structure which is the headquarters for the Smithsonian Institution. Inside is the tomb of James Smithson, the founder of the Smithsonian.

National Air and Space Museum Here you can learn all about airplanes and aerospace technology. Special exhibits include the Wright brothers' plane flown at Kittyhawk; Charles Lindbergh's *Spirit of St. Louis*; and the *Friendship* 7 space capsule.

National Gallery of Art This great museum displays paintings, sculpture, and decorative arts from throughout the history of Western art. Be sure to stand in the center court of the East Building to watch the Alexander Calder mobile move.

National Museum of African Art This museum, which is completely underground, contains one of the world's best collections of ancient and modern African art and artifacts. Highlights include textiles and carved ivory.

Arthur M. Sackler Gallery This collection contains masterpieces of ancient and modern Asian art. Chinese work in carved jade and lacquer, stone and bronze sculptures from Southeast Asia, paper scrolls and paintings, and a rare collection of Persian miniatures are some of the treasures in this museum.

National Museum of Women in the Arts This museum celebrates the contributions of women artists from the Renaissance to the present. Painters in the permanent collection include Mary Cassatt, Georgia O'Keeffe, and Helen Frankenthaler.

Hirshhorn Museum and Sculpture Garden This round building filled with contemporary art from the 19th and 20th centuries is noted for the outdoor sculpture garden below the museum.

U.S. Department of Interior Museum Visitors come to this museum for a historical view of the American West and to see displays of Native American artifacts.

Ford's Theatre This theater has been restored to look as it did when President Abraham Lincoln was shot there by John Wilkes Booth. The basement museum houses exhibits about the assassination, including the pistol used by Booth and the flag that was draped over Lincoln's coffin.

Ford's Theatre

Frederick Douglass Memorial Home You can visit the last home of Frederick Douglass, who is often referred to as the father of the black civil rights movement. The house is decorated with furnishings from when Douglass lived. The home contains his vast library, including gifts from President Abraham Lincoln and author Harriet Beecher Stowe.

Bethune Museum and Archives Mary McLeod Bethune, a black educator and women's rights advocate, advised President Franklin Roosevelt. Documents that trace the development of the black women's movement are housed in this museum, which was the headquarters of the National Council of Negro Women, an organization founded by Bethune.

Anacostia Museum This new museum honors African-American history with varied exhibitions on significant historical events and the achievements of great black Americans. It also has displays about the Anacostia neighborhood where it is located.

Washington Cathedral This huge Gothic cathedral—one of the world's largest—is renowned for its brilliant stained glass windows. The cathedral tower contains 53 bells, which ring every Sunday afternoon. You can attend a workshop to make a brass plate rubbing of medieval figures.

Dumbarton Oaks This splendid mansion with its expansive grounds and gardens is a quiet and restful place in the middle of the hustle and bustle of the city. Its museum contains an outstanding collection of Byzantine art and pre-Columbian art treasures.

John F. Kennedy Center for the Performing Arts A living memorial to the late president, this versatile arts center provides space for all kinds of performing arts. You can see plays, operas, ballets, musicals, and symphony and popular concerts.

U.S. Holocaust Memorial Museum This museum houses exhibits that honor the six million Jews and others who were murdered by the Nazis. A special exhibit presents events of the time from a child's point of view.

Library of Congress This is the biggest library in the world, but it contains more than just books. For instance, you can see the world's largest collection of comic books as well as Pierre L'Enfant's blueprints of the city of Washington, D.C. Recent renovations brightened the brilliant marble staircases, murals, and mosaics.

Federal Bureau of Investigation Here you can learn about crime investigation methods and fingerprint techniques and see a live firearms demonstration.

Washington Aquarium You can see more than 1,000 aquatic species at the aquarium. Be sure not to miss the shark and piranha feedings.

Bureau of Engraving and Printing Here you can watch money being made and printed. The printed money rolls off the presses in large sheets and is then cut into individual bills. This bureau manufactures currency, postage stamps, and special White House invitations.

Albert Einstein Statue You can climb into the lap of this great scientist. Maybe you can hear the universe spinning in his head.

National Zoological Park The highlights of this zoo are the famous panda bear Hsing-Hsing, a gift from the Chinese government in 1972, and another celebrity bear, Smokey the Bear.

FIND OUT MORE

Want to know more about Washington? Check the library or bookstore for these titles:

BOOKS

Bluestone, Carol, and Susan Irwin. *Washington D.C. Guidebook for Kids.* Washington, D.C.: Noodle Press, 1976.

Brown, Howard. *D.C. Almanac.* Washington, D.C.: Diamond City Press, 1994.

Dash, Leon. *Rosa Lee: A Mother and her Family in Urban America.* New York: BasicBooks, 1996.

Ensign, Clint. *Inscriptions of a Nation.* Washington, D.C.: Congressional Quarterly, 1994.

Epstein, Sam, and Beryl Epstein. *Washington, D.C.—The Nation's Capital.* New York: Franklin Watts, 1981.

Hoig, Stan. *A Capital for the Nation.* New York: Cobblehill Books, 1990.

Jaffe, Harry, and Tom Sherwood. *Dream City.* New York: Simon & Schuster, 1994.

Kent, Deborah. *America the Beautiful: Washington, D.C.* Chicago: Childrens Press, 1991.

Loewen, Nancy. *Washington, D.C.* Vero Beach, FL: Rourke Enterprises, 1989.

Moore, John L. *Speaking of Washington: Facts, Firsts, and Folklore.* Washington, D.C.: Congressional Quarterly, 1993.

Prolman, Marilyn. *The Story of the Capitol.* Chicago: Childrens Press, 1969.

Reef, Catherine. *Washington, D.C.* Minneapolis: Dillon Press, 1990.

Stein, Conrad. *The Burning of Washington.* Chicago: Childrens Press, 1984.

VIDEOS

Monument to Freedom: The People's House. New York: A&E Home Video, 1995. 50 minutes.

The Story of Washington, D.C. Chicago: Questar Video, 1992. 50 minutes.

WEBSITES

The District: A complete online guide. Http://www.thedistrict.com

Virtual tour of Washington, D.C. Http://www.ppsa.com/ppsa/graphics/T15/T15a.html

Welcome to the Capital of the U.S.A. Http://

INDEX

Page numbers for illustrations, charts, and graphs, are in boldface.